Holy Shift!

Recovering from Christianity with the Help of Jesus

Rev. Randol Batson

BALBOA.
PRESS

A DIVISION OF HAY HOUSE

Balboa Press books may be ordered through booksellers or by contacting:

Balboa Press
A Division of Hay House
1663 Liberty Drive
Bloomington, IN 47403
www.balboapress.com
1-(877) 407-4847

Printed in the United States of America.

ISBN: 978-1-4525-8071-5 (sc)
ISBN: 978-1-4525-8072-2 (e)

Balboa Press rev. date: 9/11/2013

This book is typeset in Adobe® Garamond Pro and Insignia Alternate.

Cover and book interior design by: Russell Phillips, The Creative Source
(www.the-creative-source.com)

This book is dedicated to all who struggle with the party line of organized Christianity—sincere seekers and rebellious souls.

Commendations

"Holy Shift!" This book is a fabulous and fascinating read for anyone recovering, or struggling for freedom, from the cult of organized religion; particularly, widespread, fear-based, versions of Christianity that distort the teachings of Jesus and squeeze life out of his beautiful message of love and freedom, leaving a load of guilt, bondage, and spiritless rules that encourage denial and suppression. Rev. Randy shakes the chains of dogma, politics, and unquestioned traditions from Christianity, and offers joyous, liberating insights into the kingdom of heaven Jesus promised is available to all who seek with a sincere heart, regardless of membership in any exclusive church or country club. Jesus said "Behold, the kingdom of heaven is at hand." Read this book and realize you are already there.

Scott Kalechstein Grace – author of TEACH ME HOW TO LOVE

HOLY SHIFT! RECOVERRING FROM CHRISTIANITY WITH THE HELP OF JESUS is a doorway to hope for those who struggle with dogma; who seek freedom from the structure and limitations often imposed by traditional belief systems. Rev. Batson's message is gentle but powerful. Grounded in the highest doctrines of Christianity, the compelling insights in his book are delivered with the expert touch of a truly inspired teacher. My highest praise goes to Rev. Batson for this wise, wonderful, and enlightening book.

Annette Childs, Ph.D. – author of SOUL MESSENGER

If you were raised in a dogmatic religious environment where God sits in judgment on a heavenly throne with Jesus by his side – one where the devil is to be feared – and if you long for a more realistic and authentic understanding of God, HOLY SHIFT…is the book for you. Your spirit will soar as you abandon archaic superstition, release ecclesiastical guilt, and embrace hope-filled, enlightened consciousness.

Royce P. Moore, Ph.D., Escondido, California

I discovered Rev. Batson's book, Holy Shift, in what I consider to be a most unlikely place, the spiritual healing community of "John of God" in Abadania, Brazil. This book is an out of the box writing that does not fit the stereotype of Christian theology in the minds of most people. Though a Catholic cleric, the author is, like myself, a former Southern Baptist, the denomination which I served as a minister for fourteen years. How far we both have moved from those days when we were defined by our religion, rather than identified by our spirituality.

As an author of a similar book, *Religious Lies – Religious Truths*, I found myself in complete sync with Rev. Batson's thesis. His book is more experiential; whereas mine is academic. In a conversational style, the author engages the reader in a dialogue about the need to return to the original teachings of Jesus and abandon the bureaucratic and controlling organization that has developed in his name, hence his subtitle "Recovering from Christianity with the help of Jesus". This is an exceptionally well written book that deserves the attention and readership of the large audience that Balboa Press will provide. Get it, read it, and devour it. If you have an open mind, you will not be disappointed. I give the author kudos with 5 stars for this landmark book!

Rev. Donald Jackson

TABLE OF CONTENTS

Prologue

What an oxymoron is the title to this book! How and why would Jesus, whom Christians believe to be the one and only Christ, the Redeemer of the world, and the founder of Christianity, ever be associated with recovery from his *true faith*, the one and only pathway to salvation and eternal life?

Here's another oxymoron. God who is ONE, undivided throughout all of creation—God who is Love greater than our capacity to understand—God who sees backward and forward in all directions—God who knows each and every one of us before we enter into our own mother's womb, has created billions of people down through the ages of time with fore-knowledge that most would be forever cast into the eternal lake of fire and brimstone reserved for the Devil and his angels because they were not Christian, or, more specifically, not Catholic, or Baptist, or Church of Christ, or Lutheran, or Evangelical, or you name it. More than an oxymoron, that may be total blasphemy. Yet, that is what so many of us who call ourselves Christian were raised to believe, even still believe; especially, we whose faith experience is rooted in the rocky soil of fundamentalism.

How do we reconcile it? "Oh, such things are mysteries," we have often been told. "God's ways are not our ways." Our faith leaders, our parents and grandparents have assured us that when we get to heaven we'll understand. "Farther along we'll know all about it," the old Gospel hymn resounds. In the meantime, our job is to keep on believing, making certain to follow God's word to the last letter, just as *He* dictated it to the divinely inspired men who recorded it. And, if living the life of *true faith* means judging or excluding those who do not embrace our particular brand of religious dogma, that's an authorized exception to the admonition of Jesus who reportedly commanded us to "Judge not, that ye be not judged," THE HOLY BIBLE, Gospel of Matthew, chapter 7, verse 11.

These are only a few of the ambiguities and inconsistencies of Christianity that have troubled me, an ordained minister, throughout many decades of Christian faith, personal and professional.

The intent of this book is not to convert, or to dissuade anyone from their chosen pathway. However, the BIBLE reports that Jesus said, "Except ye confess me before men, ye shall not enter the kingdom of heaven." This is a public confession of my faith journey through, and beyond, the dogma of organized Christianity, with what I sincerely believe to be the affirmation and guidance of Jesus, the one from whom Christian churches claim to draw their charter. An anthology of personal revelation and experience, the chapters of this book scratch only the surface of the more significant aspects of the Christian experience I have known. An exhaustive examination of each topic would surely be voluminous.

If you, too, are one who questions, I invite you to share this journey to higher consciousness and more secure faith. Many will find delicious fruits of hope along the way, peace and affirmation not previously known and, ultimately, security. Others will find only bitter herbs, poisonous berries, and thorns of blasphemy. Unquestionably, though, one of the greatest gifts of our Creator is personal choice—freedom *to take the best and leave the rest*. That is my personal invitation to you. May you always, and in all ways, be blessed.

Forward

In one of my earliest memories, I am singing "Make Me a Sunbeam," sitting at the age of three in the Sunday school room of a little Southern Baptist church in San Jon, a rural New Mexico village of only a few hundred people on U. S. 40, the old Highway 66. The only child of a mother, whose mother was Southern Baptist, and whose father was the lay pastor of a small Church of Christ congregation in the same community, my father's family was predominantly Southern Baptist. The seeds of my own faith were, therefore, planted in protestant fundamentalism. My mother had, as an adult, embraced my father's church, and I know that until my Church of Christ grandfather's death he prayed fervently for the salvation of his daughter and his only grandchild. A very good and righteous man whom I loved probably more than any man in my family of origin, he believed sincerely and devoutly that those outside the Church of Christ were beyond the limits of God's plan for eternal salvation.

Three months before my fifth birthday, we moved to Tucson, AZ. It was the middle 1940s, a time when American families were recovering from the Great Depression and enduring the difficulties of World War II. My father, an electrician by trade, drove a pickup truck owned by his employer, but not provided for personal use. Since my parents could not yet afford a car, my mother walked me faithfully every Sunday morning to the nearest church, a non-denominational, protestant-fundamentalist congregation where I attended Sunday school and Daily Vacation BIBLE School. It was there at age seven that I committed to memory the words of the beloved Twenty-Third Psalm, "The Lord is my Shepherd, I shall not want." It was also there that the roots of my relationship with Jesus began to grow and spread.

By the time I was eight years old my parents had gained more economic mobility, and a car with which to drive to a Southern Baptist church that was beyond walking distance. We were there faithfully for Sunday morning service, including Sunday school, for Sunday evening service, and for Wednesday night Prayer Meeting. It was there at the age of nine, while the congregation sang, "Just as I am without one plea, but that thy blood was shed for me…" that I went forth to the altar, together with my Sunday school friend Dennis, to be *saved*. Two weeks later, after the Sunday evening worship, we were baptized into the family of the redeemed of Christ.

Those childhood years in the Southern Baptist church remain near and dear to my heart. In Sunday school, the BIBLE stories were brought to life by dedicated teachers with sincere hearts and strong faith, despite the limits of their spiritual consciousness or the credibility of their personal theology. These many decades later I still hold and treasure the flash cards that were given to help us memorize significant scriptures. Summers were filled with Daily Vacation BIBLE School and Church Camp at the Baptist retreat in the Catalina Mountains of southern Arizona. It was during those years that the old southern gospel hymns wrapped their arms around my heart so tightly that they have never let go, and it was also during those years that Jesus became my intimate and constant companion. I was a faithful student of the BIBLE. Reading it was a daily discipline, and I never traveled without a copy in my bag. Somewhere amid those wonderful years I experienced what I believed was a *call* to ministry. During times of worship, or prayer and devotion I dreamed of being the preacher, leading lost souls to salvation and eternal life.

My mother taught me to pray at bedtime when I was a toddler. In my earliest memories she would kneel with me beside my bed and, with head bowed, eyes closed and hands folded under my chin, she taught me to talk to God. First, it was the ages old "Now I lay me down to sleep…." Somewhere around the age of five, however, she taught me the Lord's Prayer, and began helping me verbalize more personal prayers of thanksgiving and supplication. In the Southern Baptist tradition, extemporaneous prayer in groups or during worship was both the norm and the expectation, so I grew up with comfort and confidence praying aloud before others, a gift that has served me well throughout my life and ministry.

My entry into adolescence was marked by a crisis of faith. My beloved maternal grandfather died very suddenly the day after my thirteenth birthday. The shock of that totally unexpected event, together with the immense void it left in my life, sent me into a deep and dark cavern of pain and fear. The timing of Papa's death was most inopportune, inasmuch as I was falling under the spell of a magical, new substance called testosterone that was doing surprising and interesting things to both my mind and my body. Church did not seem to provide the answers I needed at that time. In addition, the Southern Baptist church of those days was not always a fun place for a pubescent young person to enjoy social self-expression. Dancing was not acceptable, movies were questionable, and not encouraged for children or teens. Alcohol was totally forbidden, and I can recall long discussions among adults attempting to discern whether it was really acceptable for Christians to drink coffee. Dress was always modest and, because it was during the years when makeup and costume jewelry were first deemed respectable for women, many girls were still forbidden by their parents to get themselves up in ways that were formerly regarded as morally barren—the immodest self-expressions of *loose* women.

By my fourteenth year I was increasingly reluctant to go either to Sunday school or church and, since my parents were at that time experiencing a period of disenchantment with the political and social complexion of the congregation to which we belonged, Sunday attendance became less a priority in our home. For a time, I ceased to put on my Sunday shoes, and my parents did not force the issue. The faith that had to that point been such a dominant influence in my life, however, did not go away, nor did the feeling of a *call* to serve. Several friends in my social circle at school attended the Methodist Youth Fellowship on Sunday night at a small Methodist church in our end of town, and their invitation to join them was perhaps a pivotal point in my spiritual growth.

M.Y.F. was an opportunity to socialize and worship with my peers in a far less restrictive atmosphere, as the Methodist church offered more middle-of-the-road Christianity. There I found spiritual inspiration, guidance and comfort in an atmosphere where it was safer to think for your self, and to experience God according to personal revelations of the Holy Spirit. Of greater importance for me, though, was that it was an opportunity to take a leadership role in youth activities, responding to my earlier perception of a call to ministry. By my sixteenth year I decided to join the Methodist Church. My parents were wise enough to support me in that decision and, in fact, my mother joined with me. Dad was unable to take that step, and for the remainder of his life could never bring his self to move his membership from the Southern Baptist Church, even though his faith consciousness took decidedly different turns with the evolution of my own.

I participated faithfully in the Methodist Church throughout my remaining high school years, and though when I went away to college I began to sprout my wings a bit on Saturday night, I rarely failed to fill my spot in the pew on Sunday morning. I remember more than one occasion when my roommate (also devout Methodist) and I got our tea a little too strong on Saturday night. Rotten as we may have felt, we were always in church the following morning. Through years of adulthood I have often marveled that our breath didn't knock the pastor over when he greeted us on our way out. Throughout those same years, however, I had occasion to visit the Catholic Church with friends of that faith. One, another college roommate, never failed his *duty* to attend Mass, though he often grumbled for two hours before and cursed the priest for an hour after. I frequently went with him, and then went on to the later service at my Methodist Church. Something about the mystery and the sanctity of the Catholic Church, with its candles and statues, and the ritual that was basically foreign to me, pulled me like a magnet. During times when I was feeling lost or discouraged, as happens to most students, I would sneak off to the Catholic Church near campus to offer my wounds and my uncertainty to the saints who seemed to live there, and to communicate with Jesus in a far more mystical atmosphere than I had ever known.

During those same years I took Mormon instruction at the Latter Day Saints Campus Institute, not because I had any desire to become

Mormon, but because I always felt a yearning for understanding of other religions. The student enrollment at Arizona State College, now Northern Arizona University, encompassed a large and active population of L.D.S. students who were constantly trying to evangelize to the *gentiles*. A Methodist friend fell very much in love with a Mormon girl who tried earnestly to bring him into the fold of what she believed to be the *true faith*. Because he could not imagine himself taking that step, her Methodist roommate and I agreed to take Mormon instruction with him. While that was not a pathway I could follow, what I learned during those weeks of instruction from young missionaries gave me a platform for understanding and compatibility with L.D.S. people throughout the later years of my spiritual ministry.

When, during my senior year, I fell in love with Joan, a devout Catholic girl, and ultimately decided she was the one with whom I wished to spend my life, it was not a difficult stretch for me to take Catholic instruction. Prior to our marriage in 1965, I joined the ecclesiastical institution that believes itself to be chartered solely and exclusively by Jesus. In the midst of the Second Vatican Council, the leadership of the Church was struggling to find its way through the darkness of ancient dogma and into a semblance of the light of the Twentieth Century. It was a most interesting time in which to begin my Catholic journey, experiencing both the old and the new Church, carrying religious *baggage* somewhat different from a *cradle* Catholic.

My wife and I were most respectful of our Christian *duty* as defined by the *Fathers* of the Church, and our three children were properly baptized upon each birth during the three successive years following our marriage. Because there was no place for married men in the Holy Orders (ordained clergy) of the Catholic Church, I tucked my call to ministry carefully away into the back of my mind. My experience has always been, however, that Spirit ultimately has its way, and our God is, above all else, a God of surprises. My lifelong interest in other faiths and cultures led me most unexpectedly to a friendship with the late Rev., Pearl Kerwin, a minister of some national renown, who in semi-retirement was founder and pastor of the Church of Divine Healing in Skull Valley, Arizona. We lived in Kirkland, a small, neighboring town where my business had taken us for two of the most exciting and eventful years of our lives. Ordained of the Baptist Church, Pearl was psychic and a spiritualist, a most extraordinary triad. While Joan and I always took our young children to Mass on Sunday morning, Sunday and Wednesday evenings would find the five of us at the Church of Divine Healing where, during an illness that sidelined Rev. Kerwin for about three months, I filled her pulpit in order to keep the small congregation together.

Fellowship with a Spiritualist congregation brought understanding to experiences I had occasionally known as a child when I saw people who weren't there, in a physical sense, that is. Familiarity with the spirit side of life also helped me to overcome a life-long fear of death, which was critical to my preparation for the important ministry that lay ahead. After moving back to Tucson in 1974, we complemented our Catholic faith practice with worship at the Blessed Trinity Spiritualist Church whose pastor, Rev. Howard Richards, became and remained my dear friend, counselor and spiritual brother until his death in 2005.

In the mid 1970s, during my 35th year of this life, a pathway opened for me to a future filled with unimaginable challenges, victories, heart-breaks and joys. The Second Vatican Council had reaffirmed celibacy for Catholic priesthood. Recognizing, however, that the ranks of its clergy were shrinking to numbers insufficient to serve its worldwide membership, celibacy was lifted for married men who felt called to the Holy Order of Diaconate. Those deemed worthy could enter a four-year curriculum of training and preparation for Ordination as Permanent Deacons, whose responsibilities were designed to augment the priest-hood, serving the people in a variety of ministries. I don't recall ever having shared with my wife that I had denied a call to ordained ministry given to me as a child. I very clearly remember, however, the Sunday afternoon when, while I was laying mosaic tile on the entry floor of our home, she knelt by my side and said "Don't you think it's time you talked to Father Todd about becoming a Permanent Deacon." At that moment the long-closed doorway re-opened, and I walked through. On Saturday afternoon, December 2, 1978, the grand, old Saint Augustine Cathedral in downtown Tucson was packed to overflowing as twelve brightly vested men, together with their wives and children, all singing "I Have Decided to Follow Jesus," processed the long, center isle to the altar where the men would be ordained by the Most Reverend Francis J. Green, now deceased Bishop of the Diocese of Tucson.

During my years of preparation for Ordination, it became apparent to me that the direction of my ministry was to the sick, and more specifically, to the dying. I enrolled in the Clinical Pastoral Education curriculum at the University of Arizona Health Sciences Center, and in 1982 made a professional transition from the world of business to institutional health care, first as a chaplain, and later as a manager of spiritual care continuums. In the twenty-six years that followed, the tapestry of my life was woven with unimaginable color and design. I worked intimately with people of every faith and of no faith, interacting with the ministers and leaders of their respective traditions, serving as a proxy for faith leaders who were not present; Protestant Christians of all denominations, Catholic, Mormon, Jehovah's Witness, Jewish, Unitarian, Baha'i, Hindu, Muslim, Buddhist, Shamanic, and Spiritualist. The *Holy Shift* had begun. I was privileged to experience the divine presence and power in each faith pathway, as well as much that I considered irreconcilable, even toxic, theology—the consciousness by which many believers who profess to be created in the image and likeness of God have actually re-created God into their own image.

One cannot tread water in raging rapids, tiptoe across mine fields in darkness, or pick flowers in the sunshine on lofty mountaintops, without becoming changed. All men and women expect and accept, to one degree or another, changes of body, mind and personality with the passage of time. Far less expected, however, and often more frightening, is a change of faith and spiritual consciousness. When experiences along life's journey knock the religious foundation from under one's house of faith, the seeker must rebuild that foundation with the tools and materials provided, or sit in the uncertainty and insecurity of a crumbling shack on shifting sands. As my own foundation disintegrated, how blessed I was to have the companionship and assistance of the master builder, Jesus, who has been my best friend, my brother, my Lord, for all the years I can remember. The work is ongoing, but the foundation more firm, and the house, once a simple cottage, now rivals the stature and grandeur of Earth's most majestic temples.

"Be still, and know that I AM God," the sacred scriptures tell us. I can now say with total and unequivocal certainty that I know, and I know that I know. What I know is that *I know nothing yet*, nor does the Pope in Rome, nor any other exalted spiritual leader on the face of this Earth. God is, but the Power and Presence of God, whoever or whatever God is, and the meaning of this experience we call life, is vast and wonderful beyond our wildest imagining. "Seek, and ye shall find," Jesus tells us in the BIBLE, Gospel of Matthew, chapter 7, verse 7. As I continue to seek, every new doorway leads to another, each, often more exciting than the last.

Acknowledgements

It would be a daunting task to name the many persons whose influence has formed a life-long faith journey leading to my current spiritual consciousness: Sunday school teachers, pastors, grandparents, Diaconate teachers and colleagues, the patients and counseling clients to whom I have ministered, and a variety of *out-of-the-box* faith companions. Certainly, my late parents, Flo and Reed Batson, deserve immense credit for *indulging* my will to follow my perceived, personal calls from Spirit throughout my formative years. My beloved wife of 48 years, Joan, and our three children, Alan, Anne and Patrick, have been faithful companions on the quest, not always by choice, but nonetheless loyal. As the story of my journey found its way to printed word, the editorial insight and counsel of my daughter-in-law, Lynn (Muggli) Batson, was integral to the finished product.

I am tremendously grateful to Russell Phillips of The Creative Source in Germantown, TN, who brought it all together. Russell's creative genius and professional guidance have been immeasurably valuable.

This work is one pinnacle of a long, spiritual roller coaster ride, sometimes exhilarating and sometimes terrifying. I could never have hung on without an indomitable relationship with JESUS, my brother and my best friend, nor could I have found recovery from the dogma, and what I now believe to be flawed doctrines of Christianity, a divine healing which has formed my current spiritual consciousness and sanctified my life-long faith in God. My religion is now what I have come to understand as the consciousness *of* Jesus, rather than the religion *about* JESUS. More than ever he is my Lord. I AM blessed, and I AM secure.

Randol G. Batson

1

In the Beginning

Genesis, the first book of The Holy BIBLE, records that "In the beginning God created the heaven and the Earth." Probably every Judeo-Christian theologian would agree that the two key words in that statement are "God created..." A major problem for me, though, both as a child and as a young adult, was where did God come from? Who or what created God? My parents and Sunday Schoolteachers all tried to provide answers, but none held substance any more than the philosophic assurance that God is without beginning. All, it seems, leaned upon the assertion of the book of Revelation that "I AM the Alpha and the Omega, the beginning and the end." All, that is, until I entered the circle of Roman Catholicism where I learned most definitively "That is a mystery." No need for further questions.

For most, it is difficult to fathom anyone or anything without beginning. For everything there is a beginning, or so it would seem, in our physical world and our mortal consciousness. And, every beginning is a result of some stimulus— an action or condition. If everything began with God, then we are again faced with the question: How, or where, did God begin?

Even the world's most esteemed scientists acknowledge that there are some things for which we simply do not have answers; at least, not yet. Some things must be accepted on faith while we keep seeking. The *Big Bang Theory* that is embraced by many in the scientific sector cannot be irrefutably proven. Even if accepted as truth, the questions remain: What caused it? Where is the proof?

Endings are a clearly understandable part of the human experience. It is difficult for most of us, though, to grasp that which exists without origination. Where does one search for God's beginning? Certainly, any answer is beyond me. If there is the possibility for any such understanding, I believe it must surely be found in humankind's consciousness of God's identity, in what we know of the nature of divinity, and in what can be observed of God's behavior. Such is the substance of my own understanding that has grown from intimate relationships with other seekers and teachers, and from a lifetime of prayer, meditation, and communion with Jesus, who has always been my personal guide.

Wherever or however God came to be, it seems self-evident, however, that God's primary nature is to create, for creation appears to be what God has done consistently since time immemorial, and continues to this present day. Five hundred years prior to Jesus, the eastern mystic and philosopher Lao-Tzu, in his 81 teachings that history has esteemed as the *Tao de Ching*, profoundly asserted that the Tao, another name for God, is the *origin* of all that exists—God, the Creator.

In the Biblical book of Genesis, we are told that God created man and woman, and created them in his own image. There is much room for discussion, debate and conjecture as to what is the true image of God. From my personal vantage point, however, there is nothing more certain than that man and woman, humankind, have, over thousands of years, re-created God into their own image—our own image. Throughout the ages and across the entire globe, the image of God has multiplied, divided and evolved as prolifically as has the human species. From culture to culture, religion-to-religion, and person-to-person, the image of God has most often taken on human characteristics, with human emotions and attitudes—love, compassion, forgiveness, hate, anger, judgment, and retribution. We have called God Omniscient, all knowing, yet we have formed dogmas and beliefs that cannot possibly be attributed to an all-knowing God. The common form of prayer, supplication—telling God our needs—would imply that God does not already know them. We have named God Omnipotent and all-powerful, yet we have involved him in a spiritual power struggle, war with a Prince of Darkness. We have called God Omnipresent, everywhere present, yet we prayerfully beg him to be with us in our times of trial, and we know he could not possibly be present in the gambling halls, the houses of prostitution, the saloons, and most assuredly not in the rituals and sacred places of those who don't believe or worship as we. Many have created God to be *the great puppeteer on the clouds* who invisibly sits high above the Earth and indiscriminately pulls the strings of his billions of little marionettes. "Let's see, I think I'll give this one $ 1,000,000, and I'll make that one a leader over many. That young mother over there, the one with five little children, I think I'll cause her to be killed in a traffic accident. Oh, there's a child down there who should be ravaged and murdered by that man around the corner, and those natives who live hand to mouth on that tropical coast are disgusting to my sight. I'll send a tsunami to wipe them and their pitiful huts from the face of the planet." All this from a God we call Love.

During my years as a provider of spiritual health care, whenever I ministered to Christians who were coping with devastating or terminal conditions, I found so many whose attitudes seemed to be, "I don't want this, but if it is God's will I accept it." Or, how often when I ministered to persons who grieved the death of a loved one did I hear platitudes of resignation such as, "God needed another angel." Though comforting perhaps for many, such perspectives describe a God of human image. The sacred scriptures define God as infinite and incomparable love, and Jesus, His *only begotten Son*, as the Lord of Love. Those same scriptures are often interpreted, however, and represented by Christian theologians and faith leaders as immutable mandates that all who leave this Earth without proper eternal credentials will go before a throne of judgment from which they will be dispatched forever to a place of relentless and unceasing punishment. God who requires that we be forgiving, is himself, apparently, unforgiving. It has been my experience that persons and churches that ascribe literally to such teaching are second to none in their ability to be cruel, judgmental, unforgiving and harsh, cloaked though those attitudes may be under a guise of love.

The BIBLE asserts that, "God is love, and all who abide in love abide in God, and God in them." Yet, we dare to exclude the grace of God from persons who abide in love but do not travel our own official pathway, or march to the beat of the drum that orders our steps.

Governments and nations which ascribe their existence and power to a Divine mandate from God have throughout history, and unto the present day, waged war on other nations, killing innocent persons and decimating their culture. In the name of the same God, those who would not accept popular interpretation of the sacred truths, those who contemplated possibilities, or who engaged in practices not sanctioned by the religion or church in political power, were tortured and/or executed, often in the most heinous and ungodly ways. That familiar scenario is in our own time being replayed between America and nations of the Middle East—Christians, Jews and Muslims, all who claim to love, serve, and follow God.

Many Biblical literalists still envision Heaven as a place high up in the clouds where its inhabitants walk on streets of pure gold and bow before God, a man, who sits on a royal throne. His power, the wrath of his judgment, and his punishment are to be feared by those on Earth, even more than children may fear a harsh and merciless father.

Fear! What an important role that godless emotion has played in humankind's consciousness of God, and in the evolution of the various denominations and dimensions of Christianity. Fear of the unknown has often motivated people to seek solace and safety in churches where doubt and uncertainty was replaced with confidence that God is, and is to be feared. Fear of damnation and eternal punishment has served church leaders well in its ability to extract homage, obedience, and material substance from the faithful. Sadly, for those unable to march to the ecclesiastical drumbeat, but also unable to erase its cadence from their consciousness, fear has inhibited their experience of joy in life, and has stolen their ability to face death with peace and confidence.

The creation story in the Book of Genesis divides God's creation of the world into six days, stating that at the end of each day God observed the work of his hands and called it *Good*. Clearly, a loving God who was totally and only good would not, and could not, have created that which was not good. Reason, therefore, demands that all the universes and everything in them are to be called good—divinely ordered—a perfect beginning. It was a beginning of harmony, a beginning of peace, a beginning of love, a beginning where each object of creation was tuned to the others like an exquisite musical instrument, and all played together in the perfect harmony of the most masterful symphony.

When humankind re-created God into its own image, it was also a beginning, the beginning of division. God became like unto whatever personal image his followers could create. While God, as self, could never change, human consciousness—our understanding of God—became fractured. The by-products of that re-creation have, throughout the ages, been division, mistrust, judgment, discrimination, hatred, war, and destruction. It is the same "us and them" attitudes that so threaten our nation and our world in this present time. These facts and attitudes, both historic and contemporary, are only the tip of the iceberg that diverted me many years ago to a path away from traditional Christianity and the churches that espouse it. Like one who is alcoholic, I don't know that a life-long Christian ever finds total recovery. It is, for me, an ongoing process. Through prayerful and disciplined communication with my personal Lord and best friend, the historic Jesus of Nazareth, I have proven to myself that it is possible to slip from the manacles of ecclesiastical dogma and walk with peace, confidence, joy, and hope both in daylight and in darkness.

I have become brave enough to understand that if we are, in fact, created in the *image and likeness of God*, it must surely be safe to assume that God intends us to use the intelligence and powers of reason with which we are endowed. None could validly contest our ability to reason the equations of mathematics, to solve puzzles, and to accomplish such unfathomable feats as sending a manned spaceship to the Moon, splitting the atom, or developing the computer age and the Internet. Should that same intelligence, then, not help us to know and understand God, while, at the same time, accepting the great enigma that God is so vast and unknowable that definition is beyond the limits of human understanding? Given that our ability to reason well may, in various degrees, be hampered by personal experience and group consciousness, should we not examine, even question the nature of a God identified thousands of years ago defined and re-defined by those whose cultural experience and intellectual capacities were primitive, at best, in comparison to our own? Yet, the contemporary attitude and firm stance of many Christian churches, and the esteemed academic institutions they sponsor, forbid us to question and examine. The adamant wisdom in my own tradition, the Catholic Church, has long been that *when Rome speaks, the thinking has been done.*

What about the responsibility to worship God that religious tradition places upon us? How many have wondered, like me, what could a god who is the *All-ness* of creation possibly need, except perhaps, for we who are created in God's own image and likeness to express that All-ness? What pleasure could such a god experience in being worshipped? Is that not, itself, reflective of a god of human image? Humankind, which demonstrates such a need to adore and be adored, has created an understanding of God as delighting in our adoration. Following the lead of the pagan traditions that preceded it, the Catholic Church, the originator of ecclesiastical Christianity, developed a tradition of adoration—adoring God, adoring Jesus, and adoring his *Blessed Mother*, Mary. That tradition spread throughout the many denominations that grew out of the Protestant Reformation, and became substance of the Commandment, one of the Ten from Hebrew Law, to "Remember the Sabbath, to keep it holy." In other words, go to church every Sunday to worship God. And, if you don't go, carry a burden of guilt for the sin of omission.

Through a laborious and often painful process of discernment, I now believe to envision God in human form, demonstrating human personality, is to remain in the pre-school of spiritual experience. The Gospels record the teaching of Jesus that, "God is Spirit, and those who worship him must worship him in spirit and in truth." What do we know of spirit? We know that it is energy—invisible, non-physical reality. The science we call Quantum Physics avows that this universe is comprised of energy, an indestructible force of which all things are made. It is irrefutably shown that all of creation is, in a manner of speaking, alive, composed of invisible particles that vibrate according to an electrical frequency. Those particles that vibrate at lesser frequencies manifest most densely—the rocks of the mountains and the soil of the fields. Those that vibrate according to rapid frequencies manifest more flexibly—water, fire, the innumerable species of the botanical kingdom, and of the zoological kingdom that includes humans. The energy that vibrates to the most rapid frequencies is invisible—air, wind, electricity, and Spirit which, among its many and various dimensions, is understood to encompass disembodied life. That we do not see it under normal conditions does not negate its existence or its power. In fact, the energy that we do not see is more powerful because it vibrates at more rapid frequencies, unrestricted by physical form. Do we, without the highest and most sophisticated technology, see atoms? Yet, who can deny the incomparable power of the atom to build, to heal, and to destroy?

If it is true, as given by the sacred scriptures and dogmatic traditions of all faiths within and without Christianity, that God is Omniscient, all knowing, Omnipotent, all powerful, and Omnipresent, everywhere present, and if God is indeed Spirit, my own lifelong journey with the companionship of Jesus has given me understanding that God is the substance of all creation. The Creator is present in the created, always and unequivocally; even more than the artist is present in the sculpture, or the architect is present in the structure, for God *is* both the intelligence that created *and* the substance comprising that which *is* created. All form is a manifestation of energy, a lower vibration, visible demonstration of that which also vibrates at higher, invisible frequencies. I have come to understand God therefore, inconceivable and indefinable though God may be, as Divine Energy, nothing more, nothing less. The Energy that is God consists of intelligence beyond our current ability to understand. It knows only to create according to its own nature, and it behaves consistently according to an irrevocable and immutable pattern of behavior—Divine Law, totally without judgment or prejudice. It never varies. God is Energy that demonstrates always the same behavior under the same circumstances. Or, as my friend and mentor, the late Rev. Pearl Kerwin used to say, "God is no respecter of persons." God, being infinite, *universal* Energy is substance of, and present to, all people, regardless of religious identity, faith consciousness, or lack thereof. My understanding may be shocking, even blasphemous to persons of faith who have not dared to look beyond the closed windows of Christian fundamentalism. I know from personal experience, however, that millions of Christians struggle with the inconsistencies and irreconcilable reason of traditional Christianity. I also know that there are millions more who crave hope and understanding, but who cannot identify personally with God as He is represented by Judeo-Christian tradition.

What a different place might this world be, and how much more quality the lives of we who inhabit it, were we to understand and embrace the Apostle Paul's consciousness of God, as given in the 17th chapter of the Acts of the Apostles, verses 24, 25, 28. "For the God who made the world and all that is in it, the Lord of Heaven and Earth, does not dwell in sanctuaries made by human hands; nor does he receive man's service as if he were in need of it. Rather, it is he who gives to all life and breath and everything else. In him we live and move and have our being…" That declaration, among all its magnificent wisdom, seems to me to hold the answer to the question about the universality and eternity of God, as well as any human perception of God's need for worship and adoration. The Apostle seemed inherently to know that God neither needs nor wants our worship; rather, that God's presence and power exists to be known to us, respected by us, and expressed by us in and from that most sacred place where he is enthroned—the heart and mind of every man and woman; indeed, by all of creation.

The paradigm of God as Energy facilitates understanding of why the sun shines upon those who behave badly as well as those who behave righteously. It gives some explanation as to why, Bernie Madoff, a famous but unscrupulous financier of our recent times succeeded in amassing unfathomable wealth at the expense of those who trusted him, while honest people of faith struggled in poverty for their very sustenance. Even if lacking faith consciousness, Madoff had an inherent conscious of how Divine Law works—of how to manifest, to create, though he did not use that consciousness honorably. It also explains why the empire he built on a foundation of dishonesty eventually collapsed upon him and his entire family.

Recognizing that to strip God of human characteristics and arbitrary nature is to some persons abominable, even heretical, my purposes will be served if, in the end, those who seek will find renewed faith—one that, like mine, owns a new dimension—faith consciousness founded firmly on the certainty of an immutable and eternal God of Love, justice, non-judgment, and inclusion of all. Again, the invitation is given *to take the best and leave the rest.*

2

God the Father

How well I remember the first time I heard someone pray to *Our Father-Mother God*. I was, as a young adult, worshipping in a non-denominational church. The guest minister addressed God in a way that seemed heretical. Hair stood up on the back of my neck. God was our Father, pure and simple. The BIBLE clearly said so. The Christian traditions that had to that time formed my own faith experience would not have tolerated a suggestion that God is, or could be, anything other than the heavenly Father. Yet, even as I flinched, something deep within me cried, "Yes!" I felt, to say the least, conflicted.

Many years later I was Manager of Spiritual Care over a staff of eleven in a large, mid-western hospital. Most of my chaplains were women, several quite feminist. They seemed to delight in teasing me by referring to God with feminine pronouns such as *she* and *her*. Though uncomfortable at first, as I gradually became familiar with their little game I began to play along. With passing time, experiencing God in ways and places I had never before imagined, I began to find human gender identity less applicable to the godhead. These many years hence, I still enjoy observing the facial expressions of selected persons and audiences when I use those same pronouns in reference to God.

I suspect that many who have just read the two preceding paragraphs may be as shocked as I the first time I heard a feminine reference to God. After all, has not Hebrew scripture referred to God as *Father* from its very beginning? And, does not Christian scripture record that Jesus referred repeatedly to God as *Father*? Irrefutably so! Would he not have grown up with that understanding, having been so taught by Mary and Joseph, and by the chief priests and rabbis under whom he studied? Jesus was a Jew who lived on this earth more than 2,000 years ago, in a time when his culture was subject to Mosaic Law. God was Father. Men were head of the family and the temple, and they held every position of power in politics and commerce. In the annals of world history, though, it was not always so. Many pagan cultures that preceded the Jews, or that co-existed with them in ancient times, were matriarchal. Women held the power.

Men were subject to the authority of women in much the same way as men have subjected women in Judeo-Christian cultures up until the 2oth century, and often still try, even in this current time. It is easy, therefore, to understand how and why, from a socio-political perspective, the Jews might have been so patriarchal, even in their spiritual practices. Though the Judaic line was passed through the mother, women and their daughters were, in many ways, treated as chattel. They existed to serve man according to his various needs, and they could be stoned to death for infractions of the social and moral responsibilities men placed upon them. Jesus was executed for teaching a gospel of love for three short years. Would he have lived to teach in that culture even three days had he ever suggested to the people that God could have been anything other than male? There would have been no need for Pilate, or a mock trial in the Roman Court. The chief priests would have condemned him immediately, and he would have been taken to the pit and stoned. It has often been said from the pulpits of Christian churches that Jesus met people at the point of their most present need. Certainly, it was the need of the Jews of his time to know God as their Father in heaven.

Given the forgoing circumstances, the powerful role patriarchy has played in world culture down to the present time is certainly of no surprise. Though women hold or control a great deal of America's wealth, their equality and autonomy in politics, in social morality, and in the workplace is still largely second to men. Our legislative bodies and judicial systems comprised largely of men still exercise control over some of the things a woman can do with her own body. The division of power is far greater, however, in countries where Islam is the State religion. In such places a woman remains chattel of her husband. Her ability to achieve education is often denied, and, her role and behavior in society is controlled by men, right down to how she dresses, and to whom, and when, she is married. Infractions of the laws and mores imposed by the men of such cultures are often still punishable by death in heinous ways—stoning, hanging or beheading.

Only in my own generation has it become somewhat common for women to hold official positions in the pastorate or Episcopal leadership of the various denominations of Christendom. Those Protestant bodies that have ordained women are often divided in congregational acceptance. The Roman Catholic Church continues to maintain an official stance against the ordination of women, reserving ecclesiastical power and authority for an all male clergy. Given the power that organized religion has played in the lives of people and their governments down through the Judeo-Christian period, even unto the present time, it is difficult not to believe that the consciousness and concept of a paternalistic god has pre-determined and formed woman's position as subservient or subordinate to man.

Many men and women have been so abused, physically or emotionally, by a father or other male authority figure that it is most difficult, even impossible, for them to call God *Father*. For them, father represents someone who is harsh, judgmental, destructive, and often down right mean. In working professionally with such persons I have discovered that, even for those with high spiritual consciousness and an intimate personal relationship with God, characteristics such as creativity, compassion, love, and forgiveness are as incompatible with a father figure as are oil and water, and a stretch of imagination beyond their power to conceive. When I came to understand that God is not the great puppeteer *out there*, but is the unfathomable and infinite power and presence of love within all, I also understood that God accepts all and identifies with all equally, whether black, brown, yellow, white or red, female, male, heterosexual, homosexual, bisexual, transgender, asexual, Christian, Muslim, Buddhist, Jew, Hindu, or whatever. How affirming and liberating it is for me to know God who reveals self patiently and lovingly according to the manner each can best identify and understand.

Realistically, if God is Divine Energy as I have suggested, one might wonder how God can have any gender identity, by human standards, at least. God, by that definition, can only be androgynous, both male and female, and neither.

Contemporary teachings of St. Germaine, and those of other Ascended Masters, assign both masculine and feminine identity to God, and contemporary students of The Violet Flame understand that the Seat of Divinity is formed of God the Father and God the Mother, *the Holy Spirit,* both of whom are resident in all of creation.

When I address God in prayer, I usually say "Father," and do so mostly for the purposes of this text since I, like so many others, am generally most comfortable with that which is familiar. I have lived most of my life knowing God as Father. I have addressed God as *Mother*, however, or as *Father-Mother God*, and in conversation I have even used the pronoun *It* without guilt or shame. The mystery is that the Energy of the Divine still hears me, and still responds according to its nature. Indeed, God is the great and ultimate paradox. The more invisible *He* seems, the more visible *She* becomes—our intimate, personal, and un-fathomable God. Whether we call the invisible force that flows through the wires to activate our appliances electricity, or juice, or power, it does nothing to change its nature, nor does it prejudice its availability and behavior. In my experience, that electricity is but a microcosm of the great Energy—the mystically intelligent, supremely powerful, infinitely creative, totally loving, immutable Force I know as God.

The sacred scriptures, if authentic and true, do record that Jesus taught that God is Spirit. In fact, Jesus is quoted as having said, "God is Spirit, and those who worship him, must worship him in Spirit and in truth." Though there may be much we do not know about spirit, few would refute that, more than anything else, it is the manifestation or flow of energy. Logic has required me to ask myself, therefore, whether spirit can possibly have gender identity, and the answer is "No," or, if it so chooses. There is, after all, so very much we don't know or understand about the infinite intelligence, creativity and versatility of spirit.

This is a *divinely* ordered universe. The sciences prove more certainly each year, as continued research gives way to more "Aha!" experiences, that nothing is random or haphazard. We know that both the masculine and the feminine are present in all life forms, whether the seed that becomes the tree, or the beginning stages of a biological species. Science has proven that every human fetus goes through a phase when it shows physical characteristics of the gender opposite from the one that it will present at birth. Though a controversial and often scorned topic in most Christian churches of our time, we see a similar pattern in those individuals whose psychological, sexual identity is not compatible with the gender to which they were born. Whereas, in most males the feminine aspect of their identity is recessive, and in most females the masculine aspect of their identity is likewise recessive, there does, nonetheless, appear to be a sliding scale in all people wherein the characteristics of their opposite sexuality manifest either more or less profoundly. In some, called bi-sexual, the two polarities appear to be more equally divided. There is continued speculation as to why such things should be. Is it the result of family influences upon the child? Is it the *sinful* choice of the adult? Is it an unconscious remembrance of opposite sexuality carried forward from a previous lifetime? The extraordinary wisdom of many Native American cultures calls such people *Two Spirited,* believing they are blessed vessels of the great Father-Mother God. The answers to such questions are yet unknown, and mostly open to speculation. Recent laboratory evidence would seem to indicate the possibility of genetic predisposition. Regardless, it may be difficult to deny that the sexual duality we find in most species of life may, in fact, be an expression of both masculine and feminine characteristics of the Creator. If, as I have come to understand, Divine Spirit, God, is the only Power and Presence in all of creation, the Creator being therefore present in the created, must that Spirit not be both male and female, and, simultaneously, perhaps, neither? I love possibility thinking. Again, I hear Jesus saying, "He who has an eye, let him see…."

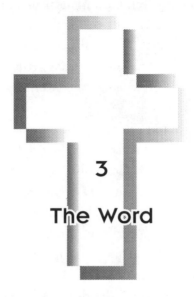

3

The Word

One of my primary challenges in the struggle to find freedom and truth amid the constraints of the dogma of organized Christianity has been the BIBLE. Having been taught that the BIBLE is, in its entirety, the divinely inspired *Word of God*, I became a seasoned adult without questioning how it really came to be. Oh, there were times when, while reading a red-letter edition of the Gospels, I would wonder how we really know that Jesus said those things. It was during my formation for ministry, however, while attending a lecture of a very *out-of-the-box* Catholic nun, that I learned some startling, historic facts that thrust me into a reality check about the sacred scriptures of Christianity, and motivated me to look even deeper.

Few would or could deny that the Old Testament, or Hebrew section of the BIBLE, is an anthology of history, law, cultural anthropology, prophesy and ancient literature specific to the Jewish people. Controversy does exist, however, between conservative and liberal Christians over the many stories contained in the various books of the Old Testament: stories such as the creation of the world and its inhabitants, the expulsion of the angel Lucifer from heaven, resulting in the struggle between God and Satan, good and evil, and similarly, the temptation of Eve in the Garden of Eden and the resulting fall of man, God's delivery of the Ten Commandments to Moses, Noah and the Ark, Moses and the parting of the Red Sea, Joshua and the Battle of Jericho, the tower of Babel, Lot's wife and the destruction of Sodom and Gomorrah, to name only a few. Are they actual historical accounts, or are they allegory—the mythology of primitive people awakening to spiritual consciousness?

For me, more questions exist in the New Testament of Christianity. Why is there such inconsistency among the records of the four Gospel writers, Matthew, Mark, Luke and John? Who recorded the words of Jesus printed in red-letter editions of those books? What about the nativity story, replete with the virgin birth of Jesus, the star in the east, the shepherds and the magi? Did the miracles of Jesus actually occur as reported—miracles such as the multiplication of the loaves and fishes, the conversion of water into wine at the wedding feast of Cana, and the raising of Lazarus from the dead? Are they, like the parables attributed to Jesus, and the famed Fables of Aesop, merely wonderful stories whose sole purpose is to communicate deeper meanings and higher truth? Why did Jesus not adamantly condemn cultural practices of his day that are totally unacceptable to latter day Christians, and to people of most faiths and cultures of our modern world—practices such as slavery, the subjugation of women, or the brutality of mob judg-ment, judgment of any kind? What about the resurrection of Jesus on the third day, and his ascension into heaven? Or, there's the Catholic doctrine of Mary having been born without the stain of *Original Sin*, her live, physical assumption into heaven, and her coronation as *Queen of Heaven*?

In ancient Hebrew times civilization had no printing presses, books, magazines or newspapers. There were no cameras, no radios, and no televisions. There was no medium for recording history beyond papy-rus scrolls and stone tablets. The most common means of remember-ing yesterday and reporting the news of today was word of mouth. As Hebrew culture developed and became gradually modernized, history was recorded more prolifically on the scrolls of the day. Much of what was written, however, was the substance of cultural folklore, and history as remembered or passed orally from one generation to the next. The official writings were recorded by an elite group of educated Jewish men called Scribes, and were normally secured within temple walls.

The recording practices of the Jewish people continued in similar ways after the birth of Jesus, and the emergence of A. D. now called the Common Era, which formed the New Testament. What many Christians do not know, however, is that the earliest texts that became our treasured Gospels which include the words of Jesus, often highlighted in red letters, were not written until approximately thirty years after his death, and many not until more than two hundred years later. Legend and word of mouth was the only channel through which those writings could possibly have come into being. Of the oldest manuscripts there are approximately 8,000, and no two are alike.

The Letters of Paul and other non-Gospel writers may be assumed to have more historical accuracy. The book of Revelation, however, filled with apocryphal, allegorical, archetypal, almost mythological imagery, and considered by Christians to be prophetic and true, may, like the Gospels, be suspect as to its accuracy, inasmuch as it grew largely from dreams and visions of a man named John during his imprisonment. There is uncertainty as to whether that *John* is the beloved Apostle credited with the *Gospel of John*, and there is doubt among Biblical scholars as to whether John's visionary experiences were recorded in a timely fashion. There was, in fact such controversy among the fathers of the Christian (Catholic) Church as to the authenticity and significance of the book of Revelation, that it was not added to the officially approved text of the New Testament until more than two hundred years after the death of Jesus.

Because these scriptures are called the *Word of God*, the presumption of the faithful and the teaching of the Christian church is that "they were inspired by God," and their recording was guided and protected by the Holy Spirit of God. The fact remains, though, that they were channeled through men who were undeniably imperfect, and who served political interests. Many had personal motives, or belonged to groups that served collective agendas whose purposes may be questionable. It has been my personal experience that many Christians who adamantly maintain Divine inspiration of all scripture will also stand firmly and certainly upon the Biblical teaching that we humans are created by God to be creatures of free will. Given the common experience of human nature, I find the two positions incompatible. While many people, myself included, sincerely believe that they are, or have been, led or inspired by Spirit at one time or another, there is no place in sacred scripture or in contemporary human experience, where it can be unquestionably shown that God ever does or has commandeered anyone's mind or actions. It would seem more clearly irrefutable that we are indeed creatures of free will, but that we may, nonetheless, be channels for Divine Spirit. Does pure water pumped through an unclean channel ever emerge as pure as when its flow began?

Reason to doubt the infallibility of sacred scripture is enforced by examination of how the original scrolls and tablets evolved to become the beautiful printed books that today we call the BIBLE. It is historically accurate that Christianity was first institutionalized by and through the formation of the Catholic Church, which existed in solidarity for some 1500 years before any other ecclesiastical, Christian body. Early texts were translated and transcribed, often many times over, from the original Aramaic or Greek and recorded in Latin, the official language of the Church, and later into the linguistics of various other cultures and nations. The translators were usually priests, or members of monastic orders within the Church, who might be presumed to have, by human nature, *manipulated* the scriptures in favor of Church doctrine. Given the political power wielded by the Church in the centuries prior to the Protestant Reformation, and the ways, sometimes atrocious, in which faithful obedience of the people was subjugated by the imposition of fear and force, it becomes even more suspect that the scriptures translated, interpreted, recorded and guarded by the Church would have been untainted or flawless by the *human condition*. In addition, there is enough variance and inconsistency in the semantics of every language that I have found it neither logical nor reasonable to presume that words always translate with exactly the same meaning.

The invention of the printing press enabled mass production of the texts that are called the BIBLE. The printing press also became an avenue for the various denominations of Christianity that rose from the Protestant Reformation to produce their own official renditions of the sacred scriptures. The preferred Protestant BIBLES have five fewer books than the BIBLE sanctioned by the Catholic Church. Some versions use only colloquial language, *thine, thou, thee,* etc., believed by many conservatives to be the true language of God, while others employ very contemporary language. A prime example can be taken from the Twenty-third Psalm, which in the official King James BIBLE states, "The Lord is my shepherd, I shall not want. He maketh me to lie down in green pastures…." A more contemporary text says, "The Lord is my shepherd, there is nothing I shall want. In verdant pastures he gives me repose…." It can be argued, and often is, that such changes in linguistics alter the validity of the text.

I remember the years when I was Director of Spiritual Care in a hospital located in an area inhabited largely by extremely fundamental and conservative Protestant Christians. On more than one occasion when, in the course of a public address I read scripture from a text other than King James, I was taken to task by one person or another for not using God's authentic Word. What they didn't know, had never been taught, is the King James BIBLE was completed in 1611 by eight members of the Church of England who edited previous translations from the Catholic history against which they rebelled. Those eight men were charged to create a version that could gain approval of Parliament and the King of England.

A preponderance of Christians, it would seem, stand firmly upon the position that the BIBLE, in whatever published text, is the infallible Word of God, just as it is written, compiled from 8,000 contradictory copies of 4th Century scrolls, many of which are claimed to be copies of lost letters written in the 1st Century. They hold the position that, though recorded by men, the BIBLE is, nonetheless, inspired by God who, most assuredly must have usurped the free will of the recorders in order to maintain purity and truth in the sacred scriptures.

Protestant Christians have traditionally been encouraged to read the BIBLE often and study its sacred scriptures for better understanding. Those belonging to more fundamentalist denominations customarily carry a BIBLE with them to church in order to closely follow whatever scriptural passage the minister may be citing in his or her message. In the more than nineteen hundred years of its history, however, it was not until the Second Vatican Council that Catholics were encouraged to own or read the BIBLE. Where one was found in a Catholic home, it was most often for recording family history—birth, Baptism, first Holy Communion, Confirmation, marriage and death. The scriptures were read to the people by the priest, and interpreted for them by the *Holy See* in Rome, which stood firmly upon the premise that *When Rome speaks, the thinking has been done.*

As one who dares to question, it seems somewhat inconceivable to me that the official word of God could have sprung from such origins and come to the present day through a historic evolution of so many variables, yet remain infallible truth, which must not be questioned. We know that in the early centuries of Catholic Christianity, there was often controversy over the validity of certain texts. Some, such as the Gospel of Thomas now embraced by many Christians, were debated and rejected by the Fathers of the Church during historic *Councils* fraught with political activity and special interest piracy akin to the Congress of the United States. The leaders of the Protestant Reformation rejected five books of the Catholic text when their versions of the BIBLE were printed. Apart from that, any difference between the sacred scriptures endorsed by the two poles of Christianity relates mainly to linguistics. I personally find it interesting that the most conservative Protestant Christians, those who stand firmly on the word-for-word authenticity of the BIBLE, are often the same who condemn the Catholic Church, which is responsible for the evolution, translation and, perhaps, biased interpretation of the books which form the New Testament.

Assuming the traditional, conservative image of a god of human form who is *out there*; the great puppeteer on the clouds, watching everything we do and pulling our strings to suit *His* fancy, leaves me with profound questions that traditional Christianity seems unable to answer. Why would such a god have *dictated* truths that are often inconsistent or irreconcilable? Would such a god entrust the validity of his sacred, infallible word to the minds, mouths and pens of flawed men who often served political bias and were sometimes even deranged;

men for whom that same word provides an easy vehicle to control the lives and fortunes of faithful and fearful masses of people, encompassing entire cultures and even governments? And, if such a creator did, in fact, give total freedom of choice to all people, are we to believe that he did, none-the-less, maintain control over the minds and actions of those who were responsible for the sacred scriptures, from the mouths of those who first spoke them, to the hands that first recorded them, to the minds that translated them, often many times over, to the editors and publishers of the 20th and 21st century BIBLES? It's a stretch too vast for my imagination.

At the risk of being branded a heretic, I must admit that, having prayerfully considered the irrefutable evidence that anthropology and the earth sciences provide, I now perceive literal acceptance of the creation chronicle to be akin to belief in any myth or literary fable, as I also do many other of the extraordinary stories in the BIBLE. That being said, I recognize a wealth of allegorical reality in scriptural chronicles.

I have often been amazed at how many Christian denominations validate their particular *brand* of faith practice by specific scriptures that may be inconsistent with or opposed to other scriptures upon which another denomination bases its reason to be. My own observation, and that of theologians who apply logic to the BIBLE, is that scripture can be found, if taken literally, to validate most anything one wants to believe.

Even so, I cannot avow my intense, personal faith in the God of the Judeo-Christian tradition, and an intimate relationship with Jesus of Nazareth who I repeatedly own as my Lord, without respecting and affirming my much read BIBLE. As I sit in my study and write, I see bookshelves that contain eleven of them, representing a variety of editions and publishers. They have been instrumental to my faith experience, encouraging me in times of doubt, comforting me in times of sorrow, and inspiring me to look beyond dogma and literal interpretation to higher spiritual consciousness—to a faith that is *knowing* far more than believing. The contradictions and incongruities which they contain have also motivated me to look between the lines and beyond the words and, in prayerful communion with my Lord, to own the freedom, hope and confidence that are often obscured by the *face-value* of sacred scripture and organized religion.

Having grown up in a literalist tradition in which the exact words and authority of the BIBLE were never to be questioned, and having spent most of my adult life and my ministry in a church in which those words were interpreted by the Vatican authority which held the official *Keys to the Kingdom*, it was very fearsome to me when I first began to question the accuracy and authority of sacred scripture. There is, however, even if one accepts the literalist claim that the BIBLE is established under total guidance and authority of the Holy Spirit, no place in the sacred book that states that it contains the totality of divine truth. My own process of reasoning and prayerful contemplation has affirmed to me the wisdom in these words of a Unity minister with whom I was once associated: "The BIBLE is the story of a people unfolding." Used as the incredibly powerful tool that it is, rather than just a literal and unquestionable compilation of history, prophecy and law, I believe it is relevant to seekers of every age and time who hunger for spiritual consciousness. Unquestionably, it has been integral to my own travels across this planet Earth, and it maintains a place of high importance as the road map for my faith journey. I can, however, no longer stand upon it or hide behind it, as do so many contemporary Christians, as reason or authority to hate, judge, or condemn other members of God's vast and glorious creation.

It is often argued by literalists of the BIBLE that *cafeteria-style* Christianity is unacceptable—that those who pick and choose which scriptures they will accept, which teachings they will honor with their faith and allegiance, are standing in quicksand. I find it apparent, however, that the *father*s of Christianity have done exactly that in their literal and jaundiced interpretations of sacred scripture, and by the manner after which they have so profoundly embraced the texts that seemed a justification or mandate for their own style of religion. More so, do not BIBLICAL literalists do the same when they stand firmly upon one commandment or teaching, but ignore another?

Consider the contemporary, fundamentalist politicians, faith leaders, and their followers who would avow the Commandment, "Thou shalt not kill," while they support capital punishment, even rejoicing at the execution of a convicted felon. I never read a BIBLE that said, "Thou shalt not kill," except in the case of...." Speaking of pious politicians, some of whom are also faith leaders of national renown, my mind turns to those who claim to serve the Lord who charged us with responsibility to care for one another, but who decline to support programs that provide for social justice, or basic welfare, health care, food and education, to the poor and underprivileged. Or, as already discussed, what about those who claim to serve a God of total love, compassion and forgiveness, who claim salvation only for those who follow their particular formula, or belong to their specific faith group? Even in this 21st Century, the Catholic Church is still excommunicating members, denying them the right even to enter the Church to pray, while it teaches a God whose love could not possibly exclude anyone.

Used by one with an open mind, a will for higher consciousness, and a heart desiring closer communion with God, I believe the BIBLE to be of immeasurable value as a handbook for life—a reference source that reminds us where we've been, helps us to determine where we want to go, and gives us the tools to form for ourselves the most fulfilling and rewarding experience of every present moment. In the hands of one with a closed mind, however—a person whose life is formed or governed by fear, it can be as dangerous and destructive as any radical religion, or the doctrine of any cult.

In my personal recovery from Christianity, I have had to make peace with the antiquity and incongruence of Biblical scripture, and the literalist interpretations that first formed my faith experience. That peace was purchased with trust in the brotherhood of Jesus who always encouraged his followers to have faith. In my understanding, true faith cannot exist in the presence of fear, so it has been a long and arduous process of letting go of fear, and trusting in the personal revelations I have received as I continued to seek. How do I know they are valid? I know, because through it all, Jesus has remained my ever-present friend, a sacred presence of immeasurable worth that will be explained with detail in a later chapter.

4

The Big Tumble

Who doesn't know the story? After God created Adam and Eve, he gave them freedom to eat any of the fruits in the Garden of Eden except those from the Tree of Life. The serpent, however, aka Satan, tempted Eve to eat an apple from the forbidden Tree of Life, and she promptly persuaded Adam to do the same. Angered that they had disobeyed him, God banished Adam and Eve from the Garden, decreeing that they should thereafter struggle for their sustenance from the soil, and that Eve should bear her children in pain and anguish.

Because the chronicle of the *fall of man* is integral to the consciousness and practice of traditional Christianity, and because it is customarily interpreted so literally, it certainly had its place in my process of separation and recovery. Looking backward, I marvel at all the years I accepted that scenario at face value, and I find it amazing that so many Christians still do. It was, after all, taught by my church as God's truth, and many churches continue to do so. It is a charming story, much akin to the literary fables our parents read to us when we were children. The time came, however, when my inquiring mind and my contemplative spirit could no longer accept the story of Eve and the apple at face value. As the 13th chapter of 1st Corinthians records, "When I was a child I thought as a child...but when I became a man I put away childish things."

New Testament scriptures, if they hold any credibility, and I adamantly believe they do, lead us to know Jesus as a master storyteller. His parables always had deeper, often allegorical meanings hidden behind simplistic or face-value dramas, and it was given to his followers to discern for themselves the wisdom and truths cloaked therein. There were also masterful storytellers in the Old Testament years. Lessons are always best learned from a teacher who requires the investment of thought and reason on the part of the student. Throughout its entirety, the BIBLE is replete with stories such as the Garden of Eden and the *fall of man*—imagery designed to communicate graduate-level wisdom to pre-school students. For me, it equates to the old response of so many parents when their children first ask, "Where do babies come from?" "Oh, the stork brings them, darling," Mother replied, or "They come from under a cabbage leaf."

How dare I entertain such thoughts, or publish ideas that might lead others astray? After all, the last chapter of the Book of Revelation, verse 19, declares profoundly that, "If anyone takes from the words of this prophetic book, God will take away his share in the tree of life and the holy city described therein." That certainly sounds to me like a recipe for eternal damnation. In the Gospels, however, Jesus is credited with having said, "He who has an eye, let him see, and he who has an ear, let him hear." In another Gospel message Jesus reportedly said, "I and the Father are one," and, "If you keep my teaching, I will abide in you, and you in me." Surely, his reported assurance that, "All things that I have done, you can do too, and greater far than these..." is an implication of the Divinity inherent to, and in, all of humanity. Trying to help his people to recognize and embrace their own Divine nature, he said, "Is it not written, 'Ye are gods?'"

Returning to the premise of Chapter One, I suggested that God is the only Presence and Power in all of creation, thereby abiding and reflected in all of the created. If that is true, there must indeed be Divine Presence within each and every one of us. How can that possibly be, many would argue, because the search would surely stretch long, far and wide to find a single person whose behavior consistently expresses anything akin to Divine? Others, the minority, perhaps, might ask how can it not be so? Can God who is One, and everywhere present, possibly be divided? To suggest that God is not inherently present in each and every one of us, even one as despicable as the late and infamous Adolf Hitler, would seem to suggest duality that is totally incompatible with God. That Hitler did not know or understand the God-presence within himself in no way diminishes the truth of that presence. He certainly used a measure of that incredible, creative power; sadly, not for good, but to the end that he became one of the most remarkable and influential persons in the history of the world. His memory lives on, and his legacy, though insufferably tragic, seems to become more and more a catalyst for positive change in the world, even in these conflicted times.

My faith journey has led me to understand that the story of Eve and the apple is all about duality, not however, duality of God. The incredible allegory was inspired by the consciousness of unsophisticated peoples to explain humankind's own creation of the *kingdom of self*—ego. It is, according to my understanding, ego that causes us to behave in ungodly ways. Ego leads us away from a state of Divine consciousness and the perfect, God-centered life that the Garden of Eden depicts. Because ego manifests most visibly in our personalities and our related behavior, it would appear that, if God is within us, there must be duality. That division, however, is illusion, existing only in our own consciousness. Jesus said, "God is Spirit, and all who worship Him must worship Him in Spirit and in truth." I now understand that we who are God's children are also Spirit. We are spirit beings having a physical experience on planet Earth.

Fundamentalist Christian protests notwithstanding, my own intelligence requires me to accept the substantial body of scientific evidence surrounding the physical evolution of life. Personal experience, however, has united my understanding with people of non-Christian pathways who have understood for thousands of years that spiritual evolution is also reality. Following the premise that the Divine Spirit of the One manifested itself in various shapes, forms and species throughout all of creation, what if the spirit entities that inhabit the species we call human forgot their true identity? Misusing the power of the Creator, failing to understand the Divine Presence that Jesus called Father, might they have created for themselves what appears to be a separate identity? And, might that perceived identity, ego, not have evolved farther and farther from their Source, the One? Duality was formed, not in reality, but in perception.

A growing body of spiritual research now indicates that ego consciousness may only represent five percent of our individual mind power; the remaining ninety-five percent comprised of our divinity, personal and universal. Any truth in that determination is overwhelming when we examine the power we have given an insignificant illusion to identify ourselves and to define the nature and quality of our life experience. It is as though a small cloud floats in a totally clear, blue sky, and, looking upward, we see only that cloud.

Consider the water that forms the seas. A wave might surge and froth until it doesn't resemble the waters of the deep, yet it is no less a part of the sea. Sometimes the waters flow into tributaries, estuaries, or smaller bodies called lakes, rivers, and ponds. The water is, yet, in its elemental identity, no less than it was. Even though it evaporates, and separates into the hydrogen and oxygen from which it was formed, those two basic elements will still, by inherent design, be reunited again to become water. Water may exist on the surface of the Earth in forms we call soft, hard or salty. It may be polluted by chemicals and industrial waste, it may flow underground in unseen tributaries, or it may be the moisture we feel above us that eventually returns to Earth as rain, snow or hail. Regardless of its perceived manifestation, it is still water, and is therefore divisible only in expression or appearance, but not in its true nature. Though it became sewage, it can again be purified, whether by human design or by natural processes—God's own way.

I believe that Jesus who, by whatever names he may be called, known to Christians of all denominations as the Master Teacher, gave us the theorems and principles we need to reason and interpret the meaning of Biblical allegories such as the *fall from grace* in order to assist us in this epic journey called life, our pilgrimage to remembrance of who we truly are. At our own speed, and by whatever pathways we choose, we seek total reunion with the Creator from whom or which separation, duality, has only been the illusion of our personal and collective ego consciousness. If God is present in all and expressing through all, can it possibly be any other way? Can salvation be anything more than a return to full consciousness of the Divine Presence within us—recognition and knowing so profound and irrevocable that we are incapable of expressing any thought, word or behavior that is less than the Divine image in which we are created—God, in whom we live and move and have our being?

It is interesting to observe how the Biblical allegory of Eve, the apple, and the fall from grace has, through the years of recorded history, been played out in Judeo-Christianity and its first cousin, Islam, through the subjugation of women. Woman has been revered and treasured as a pearl of priceless worth, and she has been likewise regarded as an occasion for sin, unworthy of positions of authority in worship, in government, and in the home. After the same manner, snakes, even the most benign and domestically purposeful, are grossly feared and despised by most sensible and rational people. It would be interesting to know whether and how profoundly the Genesis story of mankind's fall from grace has contributed to such cultural attitudes.

I now believe the story of the fall from grace to be humankind's attempt to understand and cope with its feeling of ego separation from its inherent divinity. I view it as nothing more than an allegory founded on fear. If God is, indeed, love, where can be the fear in God?

Until I learned to let go of fear, as challenged by Jesus my Lord, it was difficult for me to release literal interpretation of scriptures surrounding events such as the Garden of Eden and the fall from grace. When I came to understand, however, that God dwells within all, and is not some great entity outside and separate, literal interpretations no longer held water. "He who has an eye, let him see."

5

The Law

The scriptures of the Old Testament are replete with laws encompassing religion, culture, business and commerce. The foundation for most of those laws was the Ten Commandments, which God allegedly delivered to Moses on stone tablets during a mystical experience on Mt. Sinai. As the Christian Church emerged, the Ten Commandments were also part of the foundation for its doctrine and dogma, and were carried forward to influence moral and statutory law of nations across the Earth. In my spiritual growth and process of *recovery*, I examined each Commandment from both a literal and a figurative perspective as it is recorded, as it is taught, and as it often plays out in the lives of Christians and their churches. In that process, I remembered the alleged words of Jesus that "I have not come to change the law, but to fulfill it."

While I believe those words are often taken in the context of Messianic prophecy, I hear them saying something akin to this: "I have come to take the law out of the closet of darkness, that you might understand its true meaning, and practice it accordingly."

ONE: You shall have no other gods before me.

Could it be more simply stated? What Christian, or Jew, for that matter, would acknowledge existence of or faith in any god beyond the

God of Abraham. Yet, how often do we give our lives over to the control of addictions such as to alcohol, tobacco, food, gambling, computer activities, or the various dimensions and expressions of sexuality? When those things assume such positions of power that they destroy our quality of life, and of those around us, have we not made gods of them? Consider the *star* quality with which people of various cultures have endowed entertainers and sports figures, often adoring them in ways akin to worship, and making them wealthy beyond belief for simply excelling at whatever it is they do, even though its redeeming social value may be questionable.

When we define our lives by the accomplishments of another, rather than strive to develop and validate the star quality that lies within each of us by virtue of our Divine heritage, do we not place other gods before the ONE in whose image and likeness we are created? Or, how about when we vest total power in our church or faith leaders, blindly accepting truth as defined by them or for them by others, rather than using our God given ability to question, reason and experience in order to grow in faith and spiritual consciousness? Have we not placed other authority before God who seeks expression in us and through us? Do we not "have other Gods before Me?"

And what of *Me*? If we are each created in the *image and likeness of God*, does not the pronoun for the Divine Self apply to each of us in the same way as the *I Am*? When we sacrifice personal power and highest potential to fear, slothful behavior, or control dynamics of persons, institutions, governments, ideologies, philosophies, or religions, do we not *have other Gods before Me*? Conversely, when we seek our highest good and allow others to likewise seek and express their highest good, do we not put God in first place? As I am God, they are God. To deny the inherent divinity of self does not exalt or magnify my neighbor. Neither am I exalted or magnified by my neighbor's failure to own and express his or her Divine image to the fullest.

Taking my inquiry farther outside the box, my own process of reason ultimately formed a question that became pivotal to my expanding faith. If God is ONE and Undivided, all Powerful and everywhere Present, how can there be another at enmity with God? How do we rationalize the devil, Satan, a Prince of Darkness engaged in warfare for the sacred bounty of human souls?

How often I've listened with amazement to Christians who testify to their fear and trembling before Satan. They attest such profound belief in the devil that he holds a power akin to God, and they are usually stunned when I tell them I don't believe in such an entity or force. As one who once placed power in Satan, I now state without reservation that God, and God alone, is the seat of my trust. I do not believe in any power or presence beyond God, or at enmity with God. I do recognize that energy, the force Divine, has a negative pole, and I know that pole can behave in destructive ways when people misuse it with their creative thoughts, words and emotions.

After all, the electricity that lights our cities and cooks our supper has the power to destroy us if we don't respect it and use it properly. I choose, however, to invest my faith in the power of good—God, as it were. Satan, in my understanding, is nothing more than ego consciousness carried to its farthest extreme, personally and collectively. I very much agree with the statement of a Catholic priest with whom I was once professionally associated. A consciousness of the devil is the presence of fear. *Fear is the devil*, he emphatically stated. Inversely, it might be said that fear and/or the devil is the absence of a consciousness of love.

Jesus is commonly known by his followers as the Lord of Love. With his companionship I have come to understand that in the presence of Love it is not possible to have other gods before the One known to Christians and Jews as the God of Abraham. That great commandment is one of the most difficult to keep because it requires that I love *me*.

TWO: You shall not make for yourself a graven image.

What Christian would worship a golden calf? Yet, we worship our cars, our boats, and our collections of various things. We strive to build palatial homes that bespeak our power and wealth, while every day children the world over die of starvation. We worship our bodies, and believe ourselves not to be beautiful, desirable, or worthy if we are not slender, curvaceous, ripped, wrinkle free, impeccably groomed and lavishly attired. Fortunes are spent, and countless time expended on the preservation of youth, and advancing age is something to be denied rather than embraced and respected. What of those images? Does our devotion to them not often equate to worship? I personally believe that God who dwells within us wants each and every one of us to have all the good that we can possibly have. We should all be glamorous and wealthy, and we should all delight in the things, relationships and mobility our wealth affords. It is sometimes said that Joy is the ultimate expression of divinity. We should therefore all be joyful, and experience those things that bring us joy. Jesus taught us our joy comes from communion with God who dwells within us. When our joy comes from within, we are joyful regardless of the outer circumstances of our lives, and things we truly desire come to us easily. Conversely, it may be said that our disconnection with the inner Source is what drives us to seek the things and appearances outside of self that seem often to become akin to graven images. Any who doubt need only to turn on their television sets and watch a few of the so-called reality shows.

Increasingly I am conscious that by recognizing and honoring the Divine image in which I am created, I honor God who is ONE. The more that I strive to express my own limitless potential, God who is part and parcel of my very being, the less present become the minor gods of ego-self.

THREE: You shall not take the name of the LORD your God in vain.

Traditionally, we are taught that it is not nice to use God's name in an unclean or disrespectful way, or to swear an oath against another by using God's name, and who can argue with that? The sacred scriptures also teach us that *God is Love.* Yet, continually, even in our houses of worship, we speak and behave in unloving ways. From our pulpits we judge and condemn those who do not believe as we do, or worship according to our *correct* prescription, or live their lives according to our interpretation of God's will. In our doctrines and dogmas we teach that God only admits you into his house of eternity if you are Christian, or if you skip to the prescribed cadence down the particular pathway (our pathway) that, alone, is God's way. My own powers of reasoning assure me that such behaviors and beliefs take the name of Love, God's name, in vain.

Here's a different turn on the third commandment. If we are, as the scriptures assert, created in the image and likeness of God, do we not take God's name in vain whenever we think or speak of ourselves in negative or limiting ways? "I am so dumb." "I am worthless." "I can't do anything right." "I'm a loser." All are denial of the divinity within, and therefore take God's name in vain. Even commonplace statements that on the surface seem to attest to obvious circumstances in our lives can deny the power of God that is our birthright. "I am sick." "I am broke." "I am lost." As affirmations of negativity, each is a denial of the great power of God that dwells within. Thereby, might they be said to take God's name in vain? Sadly, these are consider-ations—possibilities that I never learned in church. How often have I broken this Divine Law, and how diffcrent would have been the quality of my own journey had I been taught truth? Every moment is a new beginning, though. Each time I take God's name in vain by negativity, I become increasingly aware, and I make a concerted effort to re-form my thoughts or words. As the positive is magnified, the negative diminishes.

FOUR: Remember the Sabbath day to keep it holy.

Where in that simple commandment does it say "You shall go to church on the Sabbath day?" In ancient Jewish belief and practice, the Sabbath Law had profound purposes beyond just temple worship. Humankind struggled long and hard from sunup to sundown in order to survive. A mandatory day of rest had unquestionable health benefits. As well, it provided an opportunity for the family to stay connected, thereby strengthening the fabric of the community and the culture.

In Christian practice the Sabbath Law was instituted by the original church—Catholic. When it was named a Cardinal Sin to miss church on the Sabbath, fear became a powerful tool for the clergy to keep the faithful coming back with their gifts and their obedience. Sabbath worship was carried forward after the Protestant churches were formed, although, as it has evolved throughout the ensuing 500 plus years, only a few hold the Catholic doctrine that failure to attend Sabbath services constitutes grave sin.

Personally, I have grown to know that there is a powerful sense of community when people of like consciousness come together, seeking to experience the Divine. Some of my happiest and most fulfilling moments have been spent in worship and celebration in communion with like-minded brothers and sisters of the family of God. At best, the wisdom of the pastors and teachers has been, for me, a vital source of inspiration and spiritual growth. I'm often reminded, however, of the song that Roy Rogers and Dale Evans made so famous back in the 1940s, "The Place Where I Worship is the Wide Open Spaces." It has been my great fortune to live and work with many whose Sabbath days are habitually spent plowing fields, herding livestock, hiking in the woods, or fishing the lakes and streams of America, and it has often been my privilege to officiate at the final services of such people. Many survivors, family and friends, have expressed comfort and hope from my assurance from the pulpit or grave site that some of the most Godly people I have ever known never darkened the doorways of churches. Jesus taught a gospel of freedom. Any ecclesiastical institution or religion that mandates Sabbath attendance under the penalty of divine judgment usurps the freedom that is ours by divine right.

How many *holy* Sabbaths I have known while walking in the woods, or riding horseback in the desert, just me, and God within me! How many *holy* Sabbaths I have known just curled up with an inspirational book in my patio, or my den! How many *holy* Sabbaths I have known in the leisurely company of good friends, laughing, sharing, and expressing the internal joy that is divine! Many of my most sacred Sabbaths have been days other than Sunday. That day is, after all, simply the seventh day on the Gregorian calendar. The creation chronicle in Genesis says that on the seventh day God rested. The ancient Jews designated that seventh day as the Sabbath, although, according to the Jewish calendar, the Sabbath day was, and still is, Saturday. That in Christian tradition the Sabbath day is Sunday is simply the work of man. I have experienced many restful, inspirational and totally sacred Sabbath days on Monday through Saturday. It took me a lot of years, though, to recognize that, and to embrace it without guilt.

FIVE: Honor your father and your mother.

Who can argue with the wisdom and value of such a command? Could we find a greater character builder than to honor those through whom we were born to this Earth, regardless of the worthiness of their personal example, or their demonstration of love? How tragic, however, that many parents have usurped the power inherent in such beautiful relationship, and imposed their own will upon their children in ways that negatively impacted the quality of their children's life. Our Christian churches fail us by not teaching parents how to empower their children, simply *guiding* them wisely as they are granted freedom to experience and exercise their personal divinity. We are taught of our duty to forgive our parents for the ways they have failed us or dis-empowered us, but, sadly, how seldom are we given tools and practical applications to accomplish that essential end. Untold numbers of people, therefore, carry to their graves excessive baggage heaped upon them by mothers and fathers, even grandparents, who abused parental power and molded them by selfish intentions, fear, and negative thinking. Countless hours are spent in the chambers of therapists, and untold dollars expended, by angry or hurting persons who feel dis-empowered or wounded by their parents, and therefore seem unable to honor them consciously and intentionally.

Honoring one's father and mother must surely mean many things. In childhood, it does mean obedience, and speaking with respect. At any age, to strive for the limits of one's highest potential is certainly an honor to parents. To forgive them for the ways we feel they have failed us, and to be kind to them even though they disappoint us is surely to honor them. We also honor them by our care and attention to them in their time of need. I have come to believe, however, allowing them to hold our personal power and thereby diminish the quality of our lives is no honor to them, nor does it honor self. On the bottom line, it dishonors God.

SIX: You shall not kill.

On the surface, that seems to be pretty cut and dried. We are forbidden to kill one another. There are some vegetarian extremists who extend that mandate to animals, as well. However, it is difficult for me to go there without forbidding the killing of plants, which too, are life forms. Application of this commandment to life species that provide for our very sustenance is a consideration with which each must find personal peace. After all, we do have to eat. Having been a practicing Christian for nearly seventy years, however, it does trouble me more than just a little that we stand firmly upon the Sixth Commandment while we wage war on our neighbors, and have throughout recorded history, in the name of a God of Love and his *True Faith*. Herein lies a real dilemma. Even if we are forbidden to attack our neighbor offensively, are we not to protect ourselves, and our families? Surely, it must be so, though no caveats are given. The commandment simply says *You shall not kill*. Jesus says, in the Gospel teachings attributed to him, "If your neighbor smites you on one cheek, turn to him the other." Most of us are not there, and are probably not easily going to get there. Still, how do we reconcile it? I have come to believe, though I am also guilty, that when we support causes and campaigns that result in the death of another, however seemingly justified by human reason, we break the Sixth Commandment.

It seems all Americans were traumatized by the events of 9/11/2001, when the acts of a small organization of hate-filled, vengeful men destroyed the Twin Towers in New York City and seriously damaged the Pentagon in our nation's capitol, killing thousands. How does a nation respond to such a heinous act and maintain national security? That is an answer I certainly do not have. It remains, though, that the command is "Thou Shalt Not Kill." The response of the men who led America at that time was to wage war on another nation; a war that was later determined to be of questionable righteousness, and a war that resulted in the death of thousands more innocent people. How tragic it seems to me that war is often supported, if not overtly, then covertly, by many houses of Christian worship in America.

It troubles me that courthouses where the Ten Commandments have historically been posted are the places where juries, often comprised largely of Christians, recommend death sentences for persons found guilty of capital crimes. Many would justify it with the Old Testament scripture that mandates "An eye for an eye, and a tooth for a tooth." That is, however, in juxtaposition to the Sixth Commandment, and is also a fine example of many inconsistencies in scripture, if one chooses to acknowledge them. Certainly, many alleged criminals seem worthy, by human judgment, of execution, but how do we justify that in light of the Sixth Commandment? And, what of those who were, in fact, not guilty of the crimes for which they were executed. The records attest there are more than just a few, and many more whose guilt was questionable. How do Christians who stand upon literal interpretation of the BIBLE support, or even, cooperate in such an infraction of the commandment forbidding us to kill? Why have not more Christian churches taken a stand of opposition to such practices?

Most of us, fortunately, never have occasion to intentionally take the life of another person. However, I have come to believe that the Sixth Commandment speaks to another aspect of living that is personal to all. Think backward over the years of your life and recall how many times your joy, your hope, your peace, your incentive, your creativity, your trust, or your faith were killed by another person—a parent, a grandparent, a sibling, a teacher, a playmate, a friend, a supervisor, a spouse, a faith leader, you name it. Likewise, how many times have we killed the same qualities, even more, in those persons over whom our words and attitudes have held influence—our children, our spouses, our siblings, our parents, our students, our friends, our co-workers, our subordinates?

To refer once again to the infamous leader of the Third Reich, Adolf Hitler, history records that he bore major emotional scars delivered in childhood by his father, and scripture says "The sins of the father are passed to the sons unto the seventh generation." How many individuals have failed to reach their divine potential because they never recovered from whatever *death* occurred within them at the hand, mouth, or pen of another person? I, like you, must plead guilty. What a different place our world might be if, as Christians, we had been taught at the earliest age the height, breadth and depth of this most important law.

SEVEN: You shall not commit adultery.

Adultery appears to me to be quite subjective. What does it really mean? Are we to understand it in terms of what it meant thousands of years ago, or in terms of what it means now? Is adultery defined by the consciousness of some discriminate or particular body of believers, or by statute? What if the statute is established by the consciousness of the people defining adultery? Such statute would seem justified if designed to protect property rights and those who have not reached the legal age of consent, whatever the jurisdiction may provide. In other words, an intimate relationship may be called adulterous if either or both parties are legally committed to another person through a marriage contract. It would surely also be adulterous if one party is adult and the other has not yet reached the legal age for consent.

Beyond that, the various Christian churches seem to throw into the adultery pot a whole mishmash of other *delicious* labels and behaviors popularly believed to be immoral. Certainly, we all have a responsibility to society, to ourselves, to God, to behave morally. But, what is moral behavior? Perhaps it is better defined by what it is probably, or possibly, not. It may very possibly NOT be anything that two consenting adults, unbridled by marriage to another, do in the privacy of their own room that is pleasurable to both and harmful to neither. Many Christians will take me to task for that license. However, any scriptures they might cite in defense of more restrictive moral judgment are given to vague interpretations, or are from the cultural mores of the Jewish people in ancient times, and therefore scarcely stand the test of modern reason. How often, though, have religious judgments of the personal and private behaviors of consenting adults resulted in life-destructive guilt?

I am pleasantly reminded of a very dear friend and former colleague, the late Reverend Monsignor John Phelan, a Catholic Priest Chaplain with whom I worked during my employment at St. Charles Medical Center in Bend, Oregon. John was a somewhat brusque but very authentic and loving caregiver in his 60s who was often heard to say, "The Church needs to get out of the business of marriage and sex." What an incredibly wise man!

EIGHT: You shall not steal.

There seems to be little room for equivocation here, except in relationship to some of the suggested infractions of the Sixth Commandment— You shall not kill. Have we stolen hope, or joy, or incentive, or peace, or whatever other emotional property of our neighbor? Have we usurped and held the power of one more vulnerable than we, and how does that differ from killing? Christian seminaries have failed their students, and pastors have failed their congregants, in not teaching that there are more dimensions to stealing than just seizing the property of another.

NINE: You shall not bear false witness against your neighbor.

Irrefutably, that is one of the more important rules for a peaceful, happy life. False witness seems, sadly, to have become a very profitable business in today's world. Just take an inventory of the tabloids that fill publication racks at the registers of any grocery store, pharmacy or convenience store. Most are replete with scandalous untruths, or with wild distortions of truth about the lives of public figures the world over. Certain radio and television broadcasts and their featured hosts also owe their public prominence to the promotion of false witness. Some of the worst purveyors of false witness I have known, however, are the rumor mills and gossip trains found among the members of Christian churches. Sadly, far too many pastors, especially those with strong political bias, promulgate false witness from their pulpit positions of power. Reasonable people recognize the tabloids of paper and airwaves for what they truly are—mediums of entertainment for those who so choose, or a dishonorable ploy to sell a product—yellow journalism, if not outright lies. False witness, however, even truth generated by gossip within a neighborhood, an office, or a faith community has the power to destroy lives. Though I would again be surely found guilty, I now understand that false witness is joined at the hip to the Sixth commandment, *You Shall Not Kill*. Many among us have had our joy, our peace, our hope, or our sense of pride, honor and self-esteem killed by the false witness of another person. Do we also stand guilty of the same?

TEN: You shall not covet anything that belongs to your neighbor. (paraphrased)

Without much stretch of the imagination, it may be alleged that failure to honor this commandment can provide an open door to transgression of any or all of commandments Six through Nine, for how often might it be said that a spirit of covetousness has been the catalyst for killing, adultery, stealing, and false witness? Oh what a tangled web!

The Law of Love

If we fast-forward this discussion from the Ten Commandments of the Old Testament to the Gospel scriptures of the New Testament, and if Jesus is quoted correctly, there can be no doubt that his single *law* for life, and his commission to all people is to *Love*. "You shall love the Lord your God with your whole heart…and your neighbor as yourself." He made it unquestionably clear the whole of the Ten Commandments, and all variations or evolutions thereof, is encompassed in that one, simple but unequivocal duty: the law to love. Sad it is that Christians and their churches are often the least purveyors of love. Attend any recovery group such as Alcoholics Anonymous, any spiritual growth group, or any of the *new thought* churches and you will find a preponderance of people who have withdrawn from organized religion because of the judgment and guilt heaped upon them in past association with Christian congregations.

The experience of countless Christians mirrors my own that, sadly, a valid response to the mandate of Jesus is often most absent in Christian churches and their members. How tragic, the most unloving, judgmental and unforgiving attitudes often come from church leaders, and are even written into official doctrine; always, of course, in the name of Jesus, the Lord of Love! A blatant case in point is the late Jerry Falwell, many years one of the most prominent religious leaders in America who, during the first decade of the 21st Century, stated publicly and without shame that "If my dog was homosexual, I would shoot him." In our own time, have not some of the most prominent and public faith leaders on our national stage, not to mention front and center politicians, been found to be personally guilty of the *sins* that they most vehemently condemned? It seems human nature that we often despise in others that which we fear to recognize in ourselves. In consideration of such attitudes I'm reminded of William Shakespeare's observation that one, "doth protest too much, methinks."

Because of the dominant role of faith and religion in the lives of all people and cultures throughout recorded history, religious laws have, as already implied, been a strong foundation for the legal statutes of society, particularly in western and middle-eastern civilization. Legislators of nations like the United States of America that identify most with the Judeo-Christian tradition have found ways to *reform* many of the most basic of those laws accepted as God's own. The BIBLE is a historical anthology of culture, religion, mythology and prophecy. It has been my experience that individual believers, governments and religious groups can easily use it to substantiate most any law upon which they wish to stand. How sad that such laws are often irreconcilable with *Love*, the supreme and only law established and affirmed by Jesus, whom Christians call Lord and Christ. He made it so very plain that any law applied, practiced or enforced without love is baseless.

Any discussion of God's Law is incomplete without consideration of the immutable spectrum of Law, which, in and of itself, is God. By semantic definition, another name for Law is Lord. We are arising from a period of darkness that has existed ever since the emergence of the scientific age. Prior to consciousness of the sciences as a credible discipline, all that was known was Divine Law, defined and interpreted largely by the Christian (Catholic) church. Hence, it was basically religious law, and was often applied and enforced as cultural or societal statute.

In chapter One, I offered my personal understanding that God is Energy, nothing more and nothing less. That is in no way to diminish God's true nature and identity. Rather, I believe it magnifies God because it removes Him from the human image in which most Christians have formed Him. In the scriptures, Jesus clearly states that God is Spirit, and, on the bottom line, Spirit is energy. The energy, which is God, is the supremely intelligent Source and Substance of all that is. It is infinite in its power to create, and there is nowhere that it is not. It is Law in that it behaves according to certain changeless and immutable patterns. The characteristics of God (Divine Law) have been identified, defined and repeatedly tested by the body of academics who call themselves scientists. A prime example is the Law of gravity. Anything with a weight more dense than air will, when dropped, fall to the level of the first substance with greater density beneath it. The Law never discriminates, it never varies, and it never fails. Though the whole city of New York may be praying for me, if I step from the top of the Empire State Building I will fall to the ground unless my spiritual consciousness is so high I am able to alter the density of my physical body or even bi-locate, as a few of the so-named Saints and mystics have been known to do. Foremost in our own time may be the late Padre Pio, a 20th century priest and mystic of Padua, Italy, who had a well-documented ability to physically disappear from one location and reappear instantaneously at another. It is told that the Apache Chief Geronimo, himself a shaman of extraordinary consciousness, may have possessed the same ability.

Another example of Divine Law was identified by Sir Isaac Newton, and taught to us in grade school science as Newton's Law: "For every action there is an equal and opposite reaction." Jesus taught the same law when in the Gospels he said, "That which you plant, also shall you reap." In the lingo of our modern times we have said, "What goes around comes around." Each is a different reference to the same action of Divine Law that was identified and named *Karma* by spiritually conscious people of the Far East, as long ago as 5,000 years. It simply means that every action, whether thought, word or deed, produces a result of equal measure. Think of it as if you threw a boomerang into the air. You can be assured that the boomerang will return to you in one way or another. If your boomerang is love, or some other positive intention, it will return to you in a manner akin to the purity of that intention. If it is a form of negativity, manifested perhaps as an unforgiving, spiteful spirit, or as hatred, greed, etc., your return will probably not be something you want. It's not that God makes a discriminative choice as to how He will respond to our actions or intentions at any given time. We make the choice by the nature of our thought, word or deed. The Law cannot discriminate, and simply gives us back a response akin to what we ordered up for ourselves. How often have we received what we did not want simply by our dwelling thoughtfully upon such things, or speaking fear-based words about what we did not want?

An integral component of this discussion, and one that has been transformative in the latter years of my own life, is the so called *Law of Attraction*, which many contemporary Christians, call, with disdain, *New Age*. Rightly so, perhaps, for it was clearly taught by Jesus, who was, unquestionably, the new age teacher of his time. The Law of Attraction alludes to the magnetism of our divine power to create. "That which is like unto itself is drawn." In other words, we are basic creators of our own reality by virtue of our thoughts and our words—the basic tools of creation. Jesus clearly and irrefutably taught the power of thought and the spoken word, and emphasized our responsibility to use them in positive ways. The thoughts we entertain and the words we express *always* create, and the more we dwell upon a certain type of thought, or the more we speak similar intentions, the more powerful will be the like response. Ernest Holmes, a new thought minister who founded the Church of Religious Science framed it this way: "Where attention goes, energy flows." The power of our thoughts and words to create is infinite and immutable, whether or not we want what we create for ourselves. It is the Law. It cannot discriminate. God is no respecter of persons.

It is exciting at this latter stage of life to observe so many people awakening to a consciousness of the tremendously creative power that each possesses by virtue of personal divinity—truth so seldom acknowledged or emphasized in traditional teaching of Christian churches. How blessed are those children who today are raised in pathways that engender an appreciation for personal responsibility to use the enormous power within them for the creation of positive life circumstances, rather than a negative focus on guilt and seemingly endless repentance for sin?

I've come to understand that the reason Jesus was so adamant about the importance of forgiveness was not because some arbitrary god thinks it is not nice to carry enmity or hold a grudge against another person. It was because he clearly understood that un-forgiveness creates disease in the spirit, and that the quality of our spirit-self affects, even determines, the quality of our physical self, and of our total life experience. Negative thoughts and words held possessively within the heart are destructive to the one who holds them. It is another expression of the Divine Law of Attraction—the immutable nature of God. Lest anyone wonder, I, too, have health challenges, have even undergone surgery in response to a cancer diagnosis, and my total life experience has borne circumstances that are not what I consciously want. Through my intimate relationship with Jesus and my renegade spiritual consciousness, I am slowly becoming aware of my personal responsibility in creating my own reality, the reality I truly desire, and I am working diligently to reform the nature of my thought and communication. I am striving to change my manner of living to be more compatible with Divine Law so I can be assured of experiencing the joyous life that is my birthright—the kingdom of heaven in the here and now. Reformation is always possible, and ANY situation or condition can be changed in an instant. It only requires a change in consciousness—merging fully with the *Love* that is both the purpose for and governor of the *Law*. That task is daunting when it requires *un-learning* a lifetime of familiar and comfortable old ways, and re-programming the thought processes that govern attitude, speech and behavior.

That our faith leaders and religion teachers have been negligent in giving us even basic understanding of so many aspects of *Divine Law*, and the power with which it governs our lives, is probably a reflection of their own misunderstanding. They learned from others, who learned from others, who learned from others who failed to question or reason. Some took sacred teachings at face value. Others may actually have exercised selfish intent to blind the faithful to true understanding of the infinite resources that lay within them. Again, I am reminded of the scripture that, "The sins of the fathers are visited upon the sons unto the seventh generation." In other words, attitudes and behaviors perpetuate themselves, unless or until someone breaks the cycle. Dare we to envision the heaven that would be brought to this world, even to America alone, if only one in every one thousand people chose to break the cycle and consciously focus upon living every aspect of life in total harmony with Divine Law? Surely, Jesus held that vision when he offered the Beatitudes—*Be Attitudes*—as recorded in the Gospel of

Matthew, chapter 5. In consciousness and practice of those attitudes and behaviors of total love, where could there possibly be a need for laws telling us what we must and must not do? Were the Ten Commandments delivered to us through the lens of love that Jesus offered, I believe he might frame them in a far more positive manner; something similar to these:

ONE: You shall have no other gods before me.
You shall seek me always within yourself, where I am first to be found.

TWO: You shall not make for yourself a graven image.
You shall know that I am Spirit, formless, limitless, and irrevocable.

THREE: You shall not take the name of the Lord your God in vain.
Your thoughts and your words shall in all ways magnify the Lord your God.

FOUR: Remember the Sabbath day to keep it holy.
Celebrate every day of your life as sacred and holy.

FIVE: Honor your father and your mother.
By the quality of your life, honor those who formed you and who nurtured you.

SIX: You shall not kill.
You shall without exception, and in every dimension, honor and preserve the life of all others.

SEVEN: You shall not commit adultery.
You shall honor all your covenants, and those of your neighbor.

EIGHT: You shall not steal.
You shall manifest all that you desire from the limitless power within you.

NINE: You shall not bear false witness against your neighbor.
You shall speak only truth of one another.

TEN: You shall not covet anything that belongs to your neighbor.
(paraphrased)
You shall rejoice always in your neighbor's good.

What an incredible, divine formula for a peace-filled, joyful life!
"The kingdom of heaven is here. Enter in."
- Jesus (paraphrased)

6

The House Divided

Even as an official minister of the Roman Catholic Church, I questioned where the various Christian pathways got the divinely approved formula for correct worship. Did God, either directly or through the power of his Holy Spirit, make known the way he desires to be worshipped? If so, does a God of love and infinite, eternal vision speak only to some of his children and ignore others? Does God not hear you if you do not address him by the correct name, as I have been taught by those who call themselves Jehovah's Witnesses? Having created diversity, one might naturally assume that God appreciates diversity among his faithful, but how, then, might some claim authority as the divinely commissioned *true church*. My scrutiny of the scriptural words attributed to Jesus, and my prayerful communication with my Lord have led me to new consciousness. If God is present everywhere and in all, expressing through all and as all, how can God not be present or validated in any form of worship that expresses Love, the common denominator? Let us again remember the scriptural teaching, "God is Love, and all who abide in Love abide in God, and God in them." How can sincere, love-based, non-Christian worship not be acceptable to God when experience has clearly shown that non-Christians can demonstrate the awesome Power that *is* God. To claim that some serve other gods, as various Christian churches sometimes maintain, is again to suggest that God is divided, or that there are other gods beside the One. Either position places God *out there*, rather than within self, where Jesus clearly taught is God's true dwelling place. All such premises beg the question I have already posed. If God is ALL, how can God possibly need or desire worship?

To carry my pondering one step further, I have known many people who love deeply and express love profoundly, but who did not identify with religion, or own any consciousness of or belief in God. Yet the scripture says "All who abide in Love abide in God, and God in them." Is this just another example of incongruity within the BIBLE, or does it demonstrate another division in Christian doctrine and ecclesiastical dogma?

As one who has finally taken ownership of his divinely inherent ability, right, and responsibility to interpret and discern for himself, I can no longer accept that any god, but one of human image, would prescribe restrictive doctrines according to which *he* is to be properly worshipped. More so, I find myself continually amazed at how many so-called *Christian churches* claim sole ownership of God's will and favor, declaring their brand of faith or mode of worship to be exclusively authenticated by God. When I was finally able to acknowledge and accept without fear or guilt the *Holy Shift* that had occurred in my consciousness, I became increasingly aware of how very divided is the house that calls itself Christian. That division presents a real conundrum, for if God is the sole Creator and Supreme Power in all the universes, God must then be indivisible—all or nothing. Are all the Christian churches right, or none of them right? Consideration of the very nature of religion and its historical evolution gave the insight I needed for reasonable discernment.

What is religion, but humankind's effort to understand the nature of creation, its groping attempt to satiate the ravenous hunger that is the call of the Divine from deep within everyone's heart. History, archeology and cultural anthropology give evidence that people of every land and time have in some way sought to understand, to celebrate, and to gain the favor of the force or forces that they have deemed greater and more powerful than themselves. Those searches have evolved into established behavioral norms and expectations—doctrines and dogmas. The more primitive the culture, the more primitive seems the religious consciousness. As surprising as it may seem, the converse is not always true. In these current times, more sophisticated than any that history records, many people, even many faith groups, still cling passionately and possessively to religious consciousness that is, if not primitive, at least a tapestry that contains prominent threads of primitive understanding and practice.

Prior to formation of the Christian church, even before Judaism, there were many and various religions that today are scorned as pagan. Some were polytheistic, and most were nature-based. As in all cultures, leaders emerged—those who were more conscious, or *in touch*, with the laws of nature (the Divine) or who at least claimed so to be. It seems to be the human condition that when we hunger for power or understanding we believe belongs to another, we tend to submit to the authority of that individual. Hence, the origination of shamans, witch doctors, and priests. Hence, also, the birth and evolution of the tremendous personal, political, and cultural power religious doctrines and faith leaders have owned and exercised over the lives of humankind.

As time passed and cultures evolved, primitive practices and beliefs were usually interspersed with the emergence of new consciousness. That which was quantifiable by the test of laboratory or, at least, intelligent reason, became coexistent with the substance of folklore, fable and tradition. In ecclesiastical Christianity today we can observe any number of rituals and principles of faith that date to pagan times. The Last Supper of Jesus on the Passover Eve before his crucifixion, commemorated in all Christian churches, is played out in *sacramental churches* in a way that is long pre-dates Jesus. "Eat my body, drink my blood" is a popular congregational hymn in the Catholic Church, where the priest, by Divine authority vested in him through the succession of Bishops, blesses common bread and wine which then transubstantiates into what is actually believed to be the body and blood of Christ, elements so sacred that only in the past forty-five years have the unordained been permitted to consume the *precious blood*, or touch the *precious body* with their own hands. In many so-called pagan rituals, worthy individuals, often children and/or virgins, were sacrificed on sacred altars, and their fresh blood collected and drunk by priests as the people bowed and prayed in homage to the gods. A far more humane rite is today called the Sacrament of Holy Communion. The Eucharistic Feast, as it is called in the Catholic, Episcopal, and Lutheran Churches, is the focal point and substance of every liturgy. In those Christian churches not classified as sacramental, Communion remains a sacred, though less essential, rite of remembrance.

I doubt many Christians know that in pagan times Easter was the celebration of Ishtar, the Assyrian and Babylonian goddess of fertility and sex. Bunnies and eggs were hex sex symbols which to this day have an important role in the celebration of Easter, even for conservative Christians. After the Emperor Constantine decided to Christianize the Greek Empire, the official celebration of Easter was changed to designate the resurrection of Jesus. Then, as now, Easter was the correct pronunciation of Ishtar.

The Catholic Church's non-scriptural tradition surrounding Mary, the mother of Jesus, bears similarity to Earth Mother themes from pagan worship. Such traditions often celebrated birth or creation from a *virgin vessel*. The application of contemporary logic makes it easy to recognize that, more than glorification of virginity, such traditions may well have recognized the androgynous (non-gender) nature of Divinity. The veneration of Mary sometimes assumes cult-like characteristics among many faithful Catholics whose devotion to the *Blessed Mother* has sometimes rivaled the belief in the Divinity of her Son, not in doctrine, but in practice. I doubt many Christians know that in ancient Rome there was a holiday that commemorated the annunciation of Cybele, the virgin honored as the mother of the Babylonian messiah. The date for that celebration was nine months prior to the celebrated messianic birth. It is interesting to observe that in the tradition of the Roman Catholic Church, there is a *Holy Day of Obligation* commemorating the Annunciation of the Virgin, also celebrated nine months prior to Christmas.

Jesus, it is written, was baptized in the River Jordan by his cousin

John, who was called *the Baptist*. The various Christian churches have designated Baptism as a common port of entry into the fold of the redeemed. For some it is a Sacrament, for others, a rite or dedication. There is variation as to formula, some requiring that the postulant Christian be totally immersed in the waters of Baptism. Most require that Baptism be administered according to the Trinitarian formula—in the name of the Father, and of the Son, and of the Holy Spirit. Some have, in recent times, become more relaxed in their attitude toward the un-baptized believer. Others remain unbending in their doctrine that Baptism is a requirement for salvation after death. Many Christians do not understand that on that historically sacred day in the Jordan River, Jesus and his cousin John were practicing a ritual washing common to many Jews of his time. Ritual washings are also found in so called pagan practices that often precede the Jews. In pagan traditions of Mexico, the worship of Wodan, the father of humanity from whom evolved the name for the weekday Wodansday, now called Wednesday, included an important, baptismal ritual of rebirth. In Babylonian tradition, baptismal purification was required of any desiring to be introduced to the *sacred mysteries*.

The Catholic Mass celebrates the transubstantiation, or bloodless sacrifice, wherein a thin, round, glutinous wafer consecrated by the priest becomes the *Body of Christ*. On the surface of the sacred bread is stamped the letters "J. H. S.," for Jesus Hominum Salvator, or *Jesus the Savior of Men*. In ancient Babylon, a deity named Baal was similarly worshipped, using altar wafers honoring Isis Horus, the maternal aspect of the Egyptian trinity that denotes the mother, the child, and the father of the gods.

These afore-mentioned considerations are mere hints of the many aspects of Christianity that would appear to be reflections of pagan traditions, and are often occasions of division among Christians. Let us look at other examples that don't necessarily have a pagan root, but that are characteristics of the house divided.

The Catholic Church mandates that liturgical worship follow forms officially approved by the Vatican. The most supreme liturgy is the Mass which can be celebrated only by a priest or Bishop. In the absence of the clergyman required for the Mass, a para-liturgical service can be celebrated by a Deacon (ordained man of lesser Order, often married), a Religious (Sister of Brother), or, where approved, a duly commissioned lay person. The focus of the Mass is the Eucharistic Feast, without exception and without variance as to form. Because only a priest or Bishop is given faculties to consecrate the bread and wine, only the bread is served at a para-liturgy, and that having been already consecrated. All other parts of the liturgy, reading of sacred scripture, the Homily (sermon), and music are secondary to the Eucharistic Feast.

In protestant Christian churches, the focus for worship is most often proclamation of the word, scriptural and preached. Those churches that might be deemed *evangelical*, however, have a tradition that sets them apart from the rest of the protestant body—the altar call. It is reported in the Gospel of Matthew, chapter 10 and verses 32 and 33, Jesus said "Whoever confesses me before men I will confess before my Father in heaven. Whoever denies me before men I will deny before my Father in heaven." The evangelical churches have an altar call at the end of each service. Some allow salvation only for those who come forth to the altar to confess their sinful nature before the congregation. Respondents are joyfully celebrated as having been *saved*. If Jesus actually said the words accorded to him in Matthew 10, he certainly gave no prescription for the *confession*. I believe we are charged to consider, therefore, whether any member of the so-called sacramental Christian churches does not make the same confession when he or she goes forth to receive Holy Communion. Likewise, what of Christians who participate in a congregational affirmation of faith, as is the practice in most non-evangelical protestant churches? Let us even take the consideration outside the doors of church. How about persons, even non-religious persons, who in their daily affairs and personal relationships, live according to those standards deemed by the Christian church to be God-like?

Carrying my pondering one step farther still, I have known many people who love deeply and express love profoundly, who did not identify with religion or who had no consciousness of or belief in God. Yet the scripture says "All who abide in Love abide in God, and God in them." Is this just another example of incongruity within the BIBLE, or does it demonstrate another division in Christian doctrine and ecclesiastical dogma?

The appropriate role of women as leaders in worship and in church politics is to this day controversial and disputed among and within various Christian pathways. The ancient Jewish tradition that woman should have no place in official worship and should be segregated from man during worship in the temple, one might assume to be an evolution of the *creation allegory* in the book of Genesis, parallel to the ancient Hebrew tradition that wives were subject to their husbands, rather than equal. Regardless, it has played out in the Christian churches to the present day. The Catholic Church has fiercely guarded the Holy Orders from the intrusion of women, and has only since the Second Vatican council permitted women to participate in sacred liturgy in ways such as reading non-gospel scripture only and serving Holy Communion.

The 20th Century saw the elevation of women to positions of political and liturgical leadership in some of the Protestant churches. The advent of woman pastors has caused an exodus among members of many congregations, and even divisions in entire denominations. Interesting as it is, the most adamant objectors have often been women. I'm reminded of my own mother who, though she became a reasonably *liberated* woman in her middle and senior years, still had difficulty accepting a woman in a pastoral role, a hold over from the Christian fundamentalism of her youth. As strongly as Protestant faiths have rebelled against Catholicism, many still hold to traditions and doctrines born of Catholic foundations such as the premise that it is contrary to God's will for a woman to lead worship or to pastor a congregation. Personally, I could never deny that, during my many years as a faith leader, the best ministers and spiritual care practitioners I knew, and often the ones who seemed most empowered of Holy Spirit, were women.

In the 1960s, following Vatican II, a reconciliation hymn gained popularity in the Catholic Church. "We are one in the spirit, we are one in the Lord, and we pray that all unity will one day be restored," was sung with fervor and sincerity. I believe most of us knew secretly, however, that restoration of unity meant that errant Christians would come back to the one, true church. In the approximately fifty years since the *relaxation* of many beliefs and attitudes that are no longer socially acceptable, the Catholic Church and its faithful seem to be kinder and more accommodating of the Christians from whom they are divided. Likewise, many of the Protestant churches, which are more conservative or exclusive, seem to have found greater acceptance of their ecclesiastical root. We've come a long way, but many Christians still hold the consciousness I remember so well from my childhood. The Southern Baptist church to which I belonged was teaching that the Catholics two blocks away were going straight to hell and the Catholics were obliged to go to confession in order to avert eternal damnation if they even entered a Protestant church. I've often heard my father tell that in his youth, in the small, New Mexico community where he grew up, if he were to walk down the street in front of the Catholic Church he would always cross to the other side for fear that the devil would grab him and pull him inside. That's the way it was, and still is for many otherwise intelligent and educated Christians, Protestant and Catholic. How do we justify such attitudes in the name of a God of Love whom we profess to be One and undivided? I find it irreconcilable, and my relationship with my Lord assures me He does too. It was He who taught that, "A house divided cannot stand."

I believe personally that the same admonition is applicable to each of us as spiritual beings who seek to reconcile our consciousness with our Divine nature. Membership in any particular faith group or our profession of faith does not guarantee our entrance into the Kingdom of Heaven, which Jesus assured us is for the here and now, no need to die in order to get there.

I have come to believe the divisions within Christianity reflect the greater division that exists in human consciousness with regard to our concept of God and the truth of our spiritual nature. When we believe that God is somewhere outside ourselves, there is division. When we do not understand we are spiritual beings inhabiting a physical vehicle and, instead, focus on our physical nature, there is division. When we do not know that each and every human person, as well as all of creation, is One God expressing, there is division. When our consciousness of self and others is formed of the illusion of ego rather than the truth of Divine nature, there is division. That consciousness of division has throughout history played itself out in negative, often destructive ways in the lives of individuals, families, communities and cultures. Father against son, mother against daughter, brother against brother, faith group against faith group, nation against nation—wars, pillage, death and grief are the common, repetitive results of the *us and them* consciousness. Like the outreaching circles that form when a rock is tossed into a pool, the consciousness of division begets and begets and begets.

Christianity, expressed in truth according to its Divine nature, has the power to heal the world—to realize the idyllic prophecy of Isaiah who foretold a time when, "The Lion shall lay down with the lamb," a time when, "Nation shall not lift up sword against nation; neither shall they learn war anymore." The dualities—pluralities—that exist within the flawed consciousness expressed by the Christian church in all its various forms is as much a contributor to a divided and warring world as is any other religion, philosophy or political ideology. To express allegiance to a Lord of Love, and then use that faith as a shield to cover judgment, bias, hatred and division is contrary to Divine nature and in complete opposition to the teaching of Jesus. The overpowering presence of such attitudes and practices, which I believe to be so contrary to the will and teaching of the one who is my Lord, are contributors to the confidence with which I ultimately walked away from organized Christianity.

"A house divided cannot stand."

7

Star Wars

Those who have read Greek Classics such as the *Illiad* and the *Odessey* of Homer surely recall the tribulations and warring of the gods. Even though Zeus was supreme among the deities, he was continually involved in strategic attacks and cunning ploys among the lesser gods. Their mythological dynamics often affected the lives of the mortals on planet Earth, as is recorded in the texts of the various literary epics, and theatrics.

Not far away, a similar Divine drama became the conscious experience and tradition of the Jewish people. One of God's most glorious and powerful angels was not satisfied with his position in the realms of the heavenly kingdom. Wanting more prestige and power, he gathered those angels that would follow him and led a rebellion against God. Angered over Lucifer's disobedience and insurrection, God banished him and his followers from heaven in much the same way as Adam and Eve would later find themselves evicted from the Garden of Eden. Lucifer was cast down to Earth, sentenced to crawl on his belly and eat the dust of the soil. One would certainly not wonder long, therefore, why so many Jews and Christians are deathly afraid of snakes.

In Judeo-Christian faith tradition, Lucifer became Satan, the Devil, who inhabits a kingdom of fire and brimstone in the bowels of the

Earth, a place called hell, accompanied by the angels who were cast out with him. They seem to have evolved into a variety of demons and dark spirits who serve their master and work with him to accomplish evil on the Earth, their prime purpose being to steal the souls of mortals—yours and mine. Christianity carried the drama one step further, believing that those who succumb to temptation and decline salvation by the Lord Jesus Christ, the keeper of the only gateway to heaven, will, upon their earthly death, be transported to the *Pearly Gates* where their names will not be found in the *Book of Life*. They will then be condemned, and cast down to hell where the Devil and his demonic angels will punish them forever in the eternal *lake of fire and brimstone*. Truly, is there a mythological classic in ancient literature that is the equal of the Biblical struggle between God and Satan—good and evil?

The Divine epic surrounding God and Satan raises, for me, several profound questions. In the first place, if God *is* omniscient, all knowing, would he not have known prior to Lucifer's creation that his most favored angel would betray him and cause such havoc in the world? And, if God *is* all omnipotent, all-powerful, would he not have from the beginning destroyed Lucifer, rather than allow him to steal the souls of human kind? Even if the drama is literally factual, would a loving Father, one who knows each and every one of his children even before they enter into their own mother's womb—knows the good they will do, and the bad—would a Divine Father such as that create even one child with foreknowledge that he would one day cast it into eternal punishment? We who are parents might ask ourselves if there is anything our children could do that would cause us to withhold our forgiveness, despite how painful the infraction. For most, the answer would be "No." Surely, our love pales immensely in comparison to the Love of God. Yet, we speak profoundly and confidently of God's immeasurable Love, and then assign to Him an ungodly capacity to reject and punish.

Christian literalists might say that God does not reject. It is the sinner who chooses not to live in such a way that entitles him to an eternity of heaven. The question remains, would a God of Love create children under such conditions? I love the story of an old Cherokee who told his grandson about a battle that rages within all people. He said,

"My son, the battle is between two wolves inside us all. One is evil. It is anger, envy, sorrow, regret, jealousy, greed, arrogance, self-pity, resentment, guilt, inferiority, false pride, lies, superiority and ego. The other is good. It is peace, love, hope, joy, kindness, humility, serenity, empathy, benevolence, truth, compassion, generosity, and faith." The grandson thought about those words for a few moments and then asked his grandfather, "Which wolf will win?" The wise old grandfather replied, "The one you feed."

I now understand that it is not God who is at war. The war occurs within us and is the result of our own ego-consciousness of duality, God and me, us and them, which is described by the Biblical allegory of the *Fall from Grace* in the Garden of Eden. That war is played out in our lives each and every day and will end in God's victory only when we each choose to attain the consciousness so profoundly expressed in Jesus: "I and the Father are One." God, as I have come to know God, is only good, and not capable of judgment. It is we, our illusory ego selves, who judge. Our egos are at war with our Divine nature—eternal Spirit. Ego however, being only an illusion of mortal consciousness, cannot win.

There is also the mitigating factor of time. The traditional Christian interpretation implies that we must be reconciled to the Father and *only* through Jesus Christ, His only begotten Son, during the period of time in which we currently exist on planet Earth. There is no time in Spirit, however. Eternity is forever, and every moment of Eternity is the present moment. What if God's love was so vast and incomparable that the *doorway to reformation* was never closed? What might that mean? Beyond traditional interpretation of scripture, what other possibilities exist for the meaning of Jesus' alleged teaching that, "except you be born again, you cannot enter the kingdom of heaven"?

Imagine my surprise when, as a seasoned adult and long practicing Christian, first Protestant and then Catholic, I learned that at the time of Jesus the body of mysticism called the Kabala held a consciousness of reincarnation, as already understood by people of the Far East for thousands of years. There is disputed evidence it was Catholic doctrine until the 5th century. To my knowledge, the Vatican has not taken an official stand as to such historical evidence. The Vatican Library, however, contains significant information surrounding the possibility, even probability, of reincarnation.

The historical findings known as the Dead Sea Scrolls, which were discovered in a variety of clay jars hidden in caves at Qumran in Israel, are evidence of a group of Jewish mystics known as the Essenes, a culture that today might be defined as extremist, if not a cult, who held consciousness of reincarnation. Contained therein were written historical accounts and religious records of the type incorporated into our current day BIBLE that have been closely guarded by Jewish and Catholic anthropologists and theologians. Some of the findings have not yet been fully revealed and there is both mystery and controversy surrounding those that have. But, there is evidence Jesus' maternal grandparents, known to contemporary Christians as St. Anne and St. Joachim, were members of the Essene community and his mother, Mary, was therefore raised among the Essenes. If that is true, it is reasonable to assume that Jesus, in his youth, was influenced by and perhaps even lived among the Essenes. As *out-of-the-box* as Jesus seemed to be in his consciousness and in his teachings compared to the Rabbis of his day, that assumption is, to me, totally possible and perfectly credible. And, given some of the sharp contrasts between mainstream Judaism and Essene consciousness, I find it easy to accept there might have been conflicts of understanding among the Jews who were the founding fathers of Christianity as they struggled and volleyed for the *truth* that was to become Christian doctrine.

Was Jesus the first *completed soul*, having been reborn to this Earth through so many lifetimes that he had *overcome the world* and attained *Christ* consciousness? Could that have been a truth hidden in his declaration that, "Before Elijah was, I AM?" Ascending from the confusion of duality to unity—full communion with the Divine Father-Mother God, totally knowing his own Divinity and expressing the power that was his birthright, was he telling the people he loved that the same birthright was their own? "Except you be born again...." Who can say? In seeking to know the heart of the Master and inviting the Christ consciousness to be my own, it solves for me the dilemma surrounding a God of infinite and unimaginable vision and power, whose love could bar the door to countless numbers of souls, and condemn them to an eternity of hell. It provides a logical medium by which *the doorway to reformation is never closed*. It is also a reasonable avenue for each and every one to attain the Christ consciousness that Jesus seemed to teach is our birthright.

Religious debate and spiritual conjecture notwithstanding, there is a considerable, though controversial, body of scientific evidence surrounding the evolution of souls from Earth life to Earth life. A growing number of hypnotherapists—psychiatrists, psychologists, and others licensed to practice clinical hypnosis—have recorded accounts of patients regressed in consciousness to past lifetimes. There are records of astounding healings, physical and psychological, enabled by way of understandings attained through the regression experience. Testimonies and books written by such therapists and scientists seem to be ever increasing in number. I find it especially interesting that many are the work of those who had no particular faith consciousness or belief in any life beyond that of this Earth until their patients began, under hypnotic regression, to slip into past lifetimes. Many of those patients were also without any religious belief or faith consciousness. Often, the identities, experiences, and places described by those patients have been historically verifiable.

Having known more than one regression experience, and felt the result thereof in my own flesh and psyche, I no longer doubt or question the words of Jesus, "Except you be born again…" Nor, can I pass them off lightly as a reference to an emotional experience that takes place at the altar of some church. It has become one of the things I know, and I know that I know. It was also known to such famous, historical persons as Benjamin Franklin, Mark Twain, Leo Tolstoy, Henry Ford, Ralph Waldo Emerson, Dr. Albert Schweitzer, Walt Whitman, Socrates, Henry David Thoreau, Abraham Lincoln, General George S. Patton, and Edgar Cayce. I find it interesting that public polls show far more people hold consciousness of reincarnation, or are open to the possibility, than dare to speak about it publicly. My own knowing has become an important part of my personal recovery from Christianity, enabling me to more securely understand that God is indeed One, throughout all of creation, present in all humanity whatever their faith consciousness or lack thereof, patiently waiting for each and every ego to be transformed in consciousness and reconciled to the One.

Regardless of whether our presence on Earth is a once-in-eternity experience or a continuous, evolutionary journey on our way to permanent realization of and reconciliation with our Divine nature, I can no longer accept the premise of mainline Christianity that God is engaged in ongoing warfare with any being, force or entity. How can it be so if God *is* truly God—all-powerful, all knowing, all loving, and everywhere present? Where can any force or power of opposition exist except within the prisons of human consciousness?

In the course of faith sharing or theological discussion, it has often shocked others to hear me say that I do not believe in Satan, or any entity as the devil. I am, however, equally shocked to know how many people truly believe in such a *Prince of Darkness*. To believe in something, after all, is to vest it with power. I have often known Christians to place belief and power of such magnitude in Satan that they seem totally bound up in fear. My walk with Jesus has taught me that consciousness of fear is the absence of love. Sacred scripture, as we have already discussed, is emphatic in its assertion that God is Love. Our scientific exploration of electricity causes us to know that energy flows with both a positive and a negative polarity. I understand the minds of humankind are full of negativity, and negative thoughts often translate into negative or destructive actions. I recognize clearly that negativity exists. There is a vast difference, however, between recognition and the investment of power with belief. I believe in God alone. In God, I vest my power. God is my Power. All else is merely an illusion of ego. Any warfare, like the mythological accounts of the Greek gods and goddesses, is played out in the minds of humankind. Yes, it is true that, if scripture quotes Jesus correctly, he is reported to have spoken of Satan, and of the devil and his angels. I must remember, though, it is also true that Jesus was speaking to a *pre-school* culture of people who firmly believed in such entities. They could not have understood concepts like ego and allegory, and had he tried to introduce 21st Century logic to them, he would surely not have lived three days, much less three years. He had to meet them where they were, and communicate with them according to the ways they could understand. They were spiritual children, but as professed in the 13th Chapter of 1st Corinthians, "When I became a man, I put away childish things."

I can only affirm as before that God, as I have come to know God, is infinite, eternal Power that cannot be divided. The division occurs in the mind of humankind, no different than it does in the Christian church. I am a first-hand authority on the disruption ego can cause in one's life. I have experienced it; I have lived it. The antics of ego can certainly be like unto the proverbial devil, and the fruits of that seemingly endless struggle between the reality of higher self, our Divine image, and the illusion of lower self, ego, can seem to be deathly. God, however, remains unchanged. Love remains unchanged. Truth remains unchanged, and life is eternal. If, created in the image and likeness of God, we are divine, and then we can have only one destiny, even if it requires being *born again* through many Earth lives. What incredible fear was released the day I came to fully understand that God *cannot* cast out God.

8

JESUS

The recorded history of planet Earth knows none who has influenced cultures, governments, and the lives of individual persons so profoundly as the one called Jesus of Nazareth. Born more than 2,000 years ago, of the humblest estate in an obscure village in the middle-east, the literary record and subsequent traditions surrounding his life from birth through death to resurrection has been the source of peace, joy and hope for many, and has brought anguish, grief and despair to many more. Wars have been waged, cultures decimated, and lives terminated, often in the most heinous and torturous ways, in the name of his Gospel of love. Conversely, in his name, divine lovers such as Francis of Assisi and, in our own time, Mother Theresa of Calcutta, have, simply by their own example, disposed the minds of ordinary men and women to a consciousness of love, and have been catalysts for positive transformation in the world.

The scriptures of the New Testament of the Holy BIBLE teach us that Jesus was the *only begotten Son of God*, and *Savior of the world*. That premise has been carried forth for two millenniums by the Christian church in all its various denominations and dogmatic presentations. Traditional Christian theology maintains that He holds the keys to the Kingdom of Heaven reserved only for those who confess their sinful nature and profess faith in him alone as *King of Kings*, and *Lord of Lords*. Even more restrictive, some churches teach adamantly that entrance into heaven is restricted to *card-carrying* members of their particular *brand* of Christianity.

I fully believe Jesus was and is, as the scriptures claim, the *only begotten Son of God*. I now know that also am I; also are you, the reader, whoever you may be. We are each created in the image and likeness of God. We are each God's children. God is not, cannot, be divided. The Oneness, the *Allness* of God is present throughout all of creation. How, then, can we each one not be *the only begotten*?

I suggested in chapter 2 that a student of the BIBLE can find scriptural foundation for most anything he or she chooses to believe. It is written in more than one place in the scriptures of the Old Testament that, "Ye are Gods," a message to which Jesus is quoted to have referred in the teachings of his own ministry. Gospel scriptures are cited as direct quotes from Jesus wherein he either stated or implied all share in the *Son-ship* of the Father. He could not have asserted more clearly that all have the power to do the awesome and seemingly miraculous things with which he was credited. He always encouraged his followers to think positively, to reach higher, to claim their power and achieve their potential. My own introspection has found that message to be far more palatable than the "Man/woman, you are lower than whale poop on the bottom of the ocean" teaching often held by traditional Christianity. One premise denies the divine image, personal power and assures hopelessness for all those who are not *saved* according to the proper formula. The other encourages people to recognize and embrace the infinite, Divine Power of God, which dwells within them, and be transformed. "The kingdom of heaven is now. Enter in," Jesus said.

The teachings of Jesus seemed to imply that the kingdom of heaven is a state of consciousness, albeit, a product or creation of the mind. What is the mind? The term is often used synonymously with brain—the organ that is the seat of our thinking processes and neurological activity. Some philosophies equate mind to the soul of man. The wisest, I believe, recognize there are some things, which, at the present time, at least, are beyond our power to define or understand, except within the parameters of current experience and consciousness. Application of the *scientific method*, however, has shown that most cannot even fathom the incredible potential that is ours, much less use it. One of the greatest known minds of my own generation was the late Dr. Albert Einstein, the scientific genius who is credited with realization and interpretation of the *General Theory of Relativity* that opened the doorway to un-imaginable realities and further possibilities. Dr. Einstein is estimated to have never used more than 15 percent of his total brainpower—his intelligence potential. I dare not compare myself to Dr. Einstein, lest I feel diminished beyond recovery. Regardless, Dr. Einstein's intellectual prowess would seem to affirm the reason of those who believe Jesus was encouraging people to become intimate with the Divinity—the unfathomable power within them.

None can deny that, historically, Jesus was a Jew, and one who loved his people deeply. Having studied, prayed, meditated and deliberated over the recorded scriptures relating to his life and ministry I believe—more so I know, and I know that I know—he was a man who, by whatever means, whether through nascent consciousness or by his own spiritual discipline had come to know and understand The Source, The Father, God, and the entire practicum of Divine Law that is God in the most intimate way. He knew the Power and Presence that was inherent to his being, his *Son-ship* with the Father.

He also understood the same Power and Presence lay undiscovered within each and every human being who ever had or would walk the Earth. It was as if he was saying to his people: "Wake up and smell the coffee! God is One throughout all of creation, and God who is One is thereby One in you. You are eternal Spirit, expressions of the Infinite and ever-present One, having a physical experience on planet Earth. You struggle and suffer because you have not understood your heritage and your legacy—the truth of your being. Your present consciousness knows only duality—you/us and them, you/us and God, Earth and heaven, Earth and hell, God and Satan, heaven and hell. I and the Father *are* One, therefore, you and the Father are One. The kingdom of heaven is here, right now. Enter in today, at this very moment, and cease your suffering. Know that whatever may happen to the Earthly body in which you now travel, you cannot die. You are Eternal Spirit—sons and daughters of the Father, extensions of the One. Put away your fear. Come home, and be at peace."

Christian tradition teaches that Jesus, being the one and only begotten Son of God, was without sin—the only perfect man to ever walk the Earth. Interesting enough, scripture also holds that He was like us in every way but sin. Considering the many errors of omission and commission the people of his day called sin, it is an impossible stretch of reason for me to accept that he lived a human life on this Earth for 33 years in such a state of total perfection that none who knew him, Jew or gentile, would have questioned his Divinity. Clearly, that Divine identity was so questioned that his life was handed over to the executioners by mass demand of his own people, and he was crucified.

The scriptures assure us Jesus was *fully God, and fully man*. In traditional Christian teaching, however, emphasis is not given to the many ways in which he implied that all He was, we also are—all that He did, we too can do. And, if he was *fully man*, does it lessen or compromise his Divinity to believe that He may have known ego-based challenges and physical experiences akin to those with which we live and struggle on a daily basis? Did he not have to relieve himself of waste products of the body? Did he not have hormones with which to deal? Surely! More so, if we, being temples of God, are thereby Spirit, does it lessen the truth of our own divinity when we, through the illusion that is ego consciousness, fail to demonstrate the truth of our divinity?

Biblical prophecies of the Old Testament foretold the coming of a Messiah who would deliver his people from bondage, into a permanent era of freedom, peace and prosperity. It was believed that he would be a mighty, temporal ruler, a king whose armies would be invincible. As a pacifist whose army was a dozen undisciplined men and a handful of adoring women, who followed him along the dusty roads and hillsides from village to village, Jesus hardly filled the bill for the King of the Jews. Yet, those who found truth and hope in his message so named him. It is interesting that when he was questioned by Pontius Pilate as to whether he was the Messiah, "the one who is to come," it is recorded that Jesus replied, "It is you who say that I am." Somehow, if reported accurately, that has never sounded to me quite like an admission of guilt.

The scriptures credit Jesus with having said, "I AM the way, the truth and the life. No one comes to the Father but by me." Upon that statement has been built the traditional dogma that we have to be Christian to get into God's heaven which is somewhere *up there*—a place to which we go, if we're found worthy, when we die. After many years of an intense and intimate walk with Jesus, however, I found myself hearing more in the things he is reported to have said, and in the things I heard the Holy Spirit saying to me, than in the alleged truths the Christian church presents about him. Facing possibilities that required me to transform my consciousness of the Lord I adored (still do) was often a fearsome struggle, I share my struggle with you here, not to convert or dissuade those who are anchored in tradition, but to hopefully assuage the guilt of other believers like me, who find themselves unable to hold the *party line*, and who dare to proclaim, "It ain't necessarily so."

That being said, any who question the sanctity of scripture are well served to return to the Old Testament story of God's delivery of the Ten Commandments to Moses, found in the book of Exodus. When Moses inquired of God, "Who shall I say has sent me?" God is to have replied, "Tell them I AM has sent you." God is also to have said, "I AM that (who) I AM." Later scriptures record that Jesus said, "I AM the way, the truth and the life." In claiming that, "I and the Father are One," he seemed to claim for himself God's own name.

We, in our own time, say, "I am" an untold number of times every day. I am happy. I am sad. I am angry. I am hungry. I am rich. I am broke. I am sick. I am healthy. I am afraid. There are personal declarations of "I am," sufficient to fill an entire book. Whether or not Jesus was the *only* begotten Son, the first completed soul, or just an incredibly enlightened human being, it seems totally apparent to me that He, in his supremely high spiritual consciousness, so identified with *The Father* that He knew God's name, I AM, to be his own. If that is so, and if we, as He suggested in more than one scriptural message, possess the fullness of his power and potential, might our Divine name be also I

AM? We will examine that possibility in greater detail in a later chapter. I believe it is an important reference at this point, however, in the discussion of who Jesus truly is.

There may be only two ways of identifying who Jesus is in these times, and in all times, since his physical departure from planet Earth. The first is the traditional identity assigned by the Christian church; one of the few things that ALL the various denominations of Christianity seem to hold as common truth is that He is the One and *Only Begotten Son of God*, the singular gateway to salvation in the afterlife. The other identity simply rests in what he is to each of us personally. Each reader, each seeker, must determine that for self.

My beloved friend Marilyn told of beautiful visits with Jesus she experienced before her very untimely death at age 36. A devout, lifelong Christian of the Lutheran faith for whom Jesus was Lord and Messiah in the most traditional way, Marilyn was in the terminal phase of a chronic disease with which she had struggled since childhood. Bedfast in her last weeks, she prayed continually, and often called out, "Jesus, Jesus," over and over again. One day, she reported, he appeared to her in the bedroom where she lay. She asked him to take her with him, but he told her it was not yet time. According to her vivid accounts to her husband and her mother, Jesus came several times, always telling her that it was not yet time. During the weeks following his first visit, Marilyn began to prophesy, an ability that she had never before expressed. Among her visions of future events, she told me that I would someday become a minister, and have a very positive impact upon the lives of many people. At that time I had not yet begun any formation for active ministry, and Marilyn had no personal knowledge of the call I believed I had experienced in my own childhood. At the time of her last reported visit from Jesus, He promised her that he would come again soon, and that he would take her with him. Within only a few days, he kept his word.

Jesus is my Lord, my personal Savior, my Rabbi, my Master Teacher, my Brother, and my Best Friend. I have known him through the messages of my various teachers over nearly seventy years, through the study of sacred scripture, and through the movement of Divine Spirit within me. I dare say I have also seen him personally, with the same eyes I use to create this text. Don't bother sending the men in white coats. I am most assuredly not delirious, nor do I qualify for mental health care, though some will surely think me crazy.

Emblazoned in my memory is an event in the early summer of 1978, several months prior to my ordination, when I awoke in the middle of the night to find Jesus sitting in bed beside me, adjacent to my wife, his torso resting against the headboard of our bed and his legs stretched out between us. It was as though I had been called to awaken. I rose up and looked at him, our eyes met and I absorbed the love that his eyes communicated to mine. I lay down again, and swiftly fell back to sleep. When I awakened in the morning I clearly recalled the experience, just as if I had gotten up to visit with my wife during the night, and I was sorely troubled by the fact that I had not greeted him appropriately. A small group of especially close companions from my class met weekly to pray together, and to discuss our progress on the journey. How well I remember tearfully sharing my mystical experience with those spiritual brothers two nights later. "Why," I asked, "did I not speak to him, or thank him, or tell him how much he means to me? Why did I not ask him even one of the many questions I have about the purpose and meaning of life?" After a moment of sacred silence, one of my brothers replied, "Because you felt so totally safe and comfortable in his presence that the most natural response was for you to just lay back down and return to peaceful rest." Somehow, that fit, and even today feels very good to me.

My other most mystical and intimate experience with Jesus was around 1995, when I experienced a lucid dream so real that it affected me physically for several days. The scene was a hospital where I was apparently a patient in the Intensive Care Unit. In retrospect, that was about the time I had really come face-to-face with the fact I could no longer accept traditional Christianity, and I was already beginning to envision a book by this title. In the dream, my lifelong friend, Robert, himself a physician, pushed me in a wheelchair to the hospital chapel, where Jesus was standing at the altar. Robert pushed me down the aisle to Jesus' feet. Jesus bent down, put his hands on my shoulders and kissed me on the forehead, right in the middle of the sixth chakra, often called the third eye. My wheelchair immediately flipped upward, with me as securely seated as though I were fastened with a belt. I flipped upside down in the air and landed head first in soft soil at the base of a palm tree that had suddenly appeared in the chapel, right where the center aisle had been. I remained there for a moment, the top of my head buried in the soil and my body, together with wheelchair, suspended in the air. I was in a swoon-like state with waves of incredible joy surging through my body from head to feet. When I awoke, my body was still in a state of euphoria, and I was overwhelmed with joy and peace beyond my ability to describe. That physical-emotional high possessed an orgasmic quality that remained with me for several days. It was like I have heard others describe a *good trip* on a hallucinogenic drug, although there were no hallucinations and I was drug free. Christians who have experienced the phenomenon of being *slain in the Spirit* would have some frame of reference for what I felt, except that my euphoria was many times greater than any I have ever known and the physical and emotional high was so intense, I wondered for several days whether it would ever go away.

Alas, it did, but the relationship with my Lord was forged more solidly than I could ever have imagined. In retrospect, it was as though I had received a very powerful and personal blessing from him at a time when I was consciously venturing away from what I had always believed to be his *fold*. Those who pay attention to the symbolism of their dreams may also recognize the powerful image of *grounding* represented by my crown chakra being buried in the soil at the base of the palm tree.

Many years ago, the famous actress Shirley McClain, herself a spiritual seeker of no small renown, wrote a best-selling book titled *Out on a Limb*. I recall how the late Rev. Jerry Falwell, perhaps the most prominent Southern Baptist pastor of his era, referred to her book as, "Out on a Broken Limb." I ask myself today, as I did then, if I were out on a broken limb, would my Lord have come to me with such a profound and enduring blessing? Why would he have shown me such intimate affirmation, knowing, as he surely did, that I would eventually walk away from the traditional dogma of the Christian church?

Was he trying to hold me within the fold, or was he commissioning me for the difficult journey of faith reformation upon which I was already embarking, making sure whatever road I traveled I could not doubt his presence with me? The answer, for me, is the latter. Surely, he knew the Christian church could not contain me, could not own me, nor, I believe, did he care.

The Roman Catholic authority, by which I am ordained, teaches that Jesus founded the Christian Church, and appointed his Apostle Peter to be the first Pope. A person of faith who accepts the Catholic interpretation of the Gospel of Matthew can surely be nothing less than Catholic, for it was from those words the fathers of the ancient church drew their charter. It is interesting to me the scriptures use the word *church*. To my knowledge, there was no such thing as church in those days. The Jewish people were a culture as much as a religion and they worshipped God in temples. They were the only monotheistic faith in that geographic vicinity, at least during the time of Jesus. Did Jesus coin a new word—one to designate the ecclesiastical organization he had supposedly come to found—or was that word the invention of the men who later formed the institution that became the mother of ecclesiastical Christianity?

My own faith journey with the constant companionship of Jesus has caused me to believe that it was never his intent to form a church—any church. If Jesus' message was one of freedom through Divine Love, why would He have created an institution that would enslave the minds, the hearts, even the behavior of the people He loved? Why would He have given such authority to men He knew would usurp power, and abuse that power in the most unloving of ways: from the holy wars staged and waged in the name of Christianity, to the heinous acts of torture and executions of the Inquisition era, to harsh judgments that have destroyed the quality of life for faithful but weak persons struggling for peace with God while living with deep thorns in their flesh, to the physical and emotional abuse of young people whose minds and wills were not yet fully cast in maturity, to the invasion of privacy into its members own bedrooms? To suggest He did not know is to limit the depth of his vision and the breadth of his heart.

In my faith journey I found myself asking why He would, if He is indeed Lord and Messiah, have established such a narrow and exclusive gateway to the kingdom of God, when the lives of millions preceded the opening of that gateway; when billions more would live who would not ever know of the gateway, or, because of their own cultural consciousness could not see that gateway. What did He mean when, in the Gospels, He reportedly said, "I have other sheep that are not of this fold?" Was He referring to God's many children of various cultures and belief systems in other parts of the world? Might that even have included life in places beyond this seemingly insignificant little planet we call Earth, spinning in an immense galaxy that is, itself, only one of many in a sea of infinity? Much is not yet known, but the depth and breadth of what we do know is a mandate that we at least entertain the possibility?

Jesus is quoted to have said, "I have overcome the world." Prompted by my personal relationship with him, I hear in those words a meaning far more profound than common interpretation. To me, He says, "I have overcome ego consciousness," which, in the minds of human kind, forms the world. Therein, I know, like Jesus, "I and the Father are One," even though the presence of my ego consciousness currently designs an illusion of division. A daily discipline of prayer, meditation and spiritual study, with a mind that is open to any possibility, are the tools I use as I struggle for Divine Consciousness—the Mind of God—that is the truth of my identity, and was realized so long ago by the Master Teacher Jesus, who is my Lord.

A popular bumper sticker displayed by some Christians in the 1990s declared, "Jesus is coming soon, and He is pissed!" I cannot speak to how soon he might be coming, if indeed he is, but I am quite certain he is thoroughly *pissed*; not so much because of the sinfulness of the world, as defined by Christian theologians and church authority, but by the manner in which the various churches have usurped power, abused authority, and distorted, even recreated, his truth to reflect their own image and ego bias.

What Does "Christ" Mean?

I'm reminded of J. D. Salinger's famously acclaimed novel, *Catcher In The Rye*, which was required reading in my freshman English class at the University of Arizona. The main character, a teenage boy named Holden Caulfield, was always proclaiming, "Jesus H. Christ!" While, *Jesus Christ*, is frequently used as a profanity by those who don't make higher choices for self-expression, it is the name most commonly used by Christians in reference to their Lord. It is as though Christ were his last name. Often, the name Jesus is omitted and he is simply called Christ. Contrary to common belief, however, Jesus' last name was not and is not Christ. Christ, as I have come to know, identifies the state of divine consciousness that was fully expressed in Jesus. It might equate to the Christian concept of Messiah. Referring to the scriptures, which record the trial of Jesus in the court of Pontius Pilate, we are told that Pilate asked him, "Are you the Christ, the Son of God?" If we are all the sons and daughters of God, is not the Christ consciousness our divine legacy, a brilliant identity that is expressed, to greater or lesser degrees, in each of us? Is it not our highest goal, our common Divinity and Oneness with God, the realization of which is our common destiny? Pilate was, of course, referring to the charge of Jesus' enemies that he was the one and only. Jesus' response was, "It is you who say that I am."

When I scrutinize the scriptures, especially those where Jesus challenges his followers to go within, to embrace the indwelling Father and tap into the Divine Power, which is the core of our being, I find myself in solidarity with those students of the BIBLE who believe he implied, what we call Christ is indeed the Divinity in which we are formed and which expresses in and through each of us, whether or not we know it or use it responsibly. Certainly, that consciousness and its expression rises or falls on a sliding scale personal to each of us, and has, so far as we know, not seen the equal of Jesus in all the years since he walked the Earth. Regardless, that truth in no way negates its presence within us, and the potential He assures us is ours. Even as we have called him Jesus the Christ, might we, if we fully realized and expressed our true Divine nature, be called Rudy the Christ, or Shirley the Christ, or Becky the Christ, or (your name here) the Christ, or…?

Even if Jesus challenged us to welcome the Christ consciousness that is our birthright, and express our fullest potential, the occasions when I have succeeded in reaching that far off star have been only sporadic and brief. Still, I must believe what I have personally experienced. I wonder how many others out there would say, "I know, and I know that I know." Yet, because of fear instilled by the authority of the Christian church they continue to know in silence, and their knowing is often confounded by the ego shadow of self-doubt.

Messiah

What is a Messiah? Is it a deliverer, a savior, a protector? One who would render his or her people victorious over all adversity? Translated to English from its Hebrew root, Messiah means *the anointed one*. Anointing is a tradition that began in pagan times. Great leaders and persons of special power were considered to have been *anointed* of the various gods. In Hebrew scripture, great leaders, and often first sons, were anointed in recognition of their personal authority, or favor with God. That tradition has carried forth to modern times when monarchs are still anointed at their coronation, and religious leaders within and outside of the Christian church are anointed at the time of ordination.

The Jews before and after the time of Jesus were looking for a temporal king who would be their own—one to make them prosper and protect them from enemies who had subjugated them throughout their history. Certainly, one such as that would be the anointed one. The focus of the Jews has always been on the life of this Earth, leaving Eternity to whatever the hereafter delivers. They are faithful, stalwart, long-suffering people who have envisioned a Messiah the likes of whom has not yet come for them. Christians, early and contemporary, how-ever, seem always to have considered this life more as something to be obediently and patiently endured in order to be found worthy of the life of Eternity. They have idealized the same messianic qualities in a spiritual king whose friendship assures a safe place in the afterlife. Having taken their charter from the life and alleged teachings of the historical Jesus, He is the one they call Messiah, and their relationship with him is formed, defined and guarded through and by the Christian church, in all its various *flavors*.

Unquestionably, Jesus is my Messiah. He has delivered me from the bondage of dogma. He has revealed to me the illusion that is ego, and he has saved me from the consciousness of duality. Jesus has shown me that there is no place where God is not; therefore, I AM safe and protected at all times, wherever I may dwell in the Infinity and Eternity of God. That I may not always *get it*, or that I, having by no measure reached the ascended stature of my Lord, may seldom, if ever, demonstrate the Christ consciousness, makes it no less true. Alas, this pilgrim on a journey of countless incarnations to the human family of planet Earth is a work in progress. While I experience Jesus as the highest example and the pinnacle of my spiritual consciousness, there are those who have also been Messiah for me personally during the years of this specific Earth journey. In the broadest sense, Messiahs are many. Mother Theresa was Messiah to countless homeless people on the streets of Calcutta, whom she and her Sisters carried home, bathed, fed, and rocked in their arms of love to the safe sleep of death. Mohandas Gandhi was Messiah to the culture for which he improved the quality of life by his wisdom and his firm stance of non-resistance. The Buddha is Messiah to the millions to whom he has shown a pathway to *Enlightenment*. Faith leaders who have sincerely and compassionately offered a lifeline of hope, peace, healing and forgiveness, irrespective of their own truth consciousness, are Messiah to those who trust them. Hopefully, I have been, or will yet be, Messiah to some. And you?

9
Prayer

Prayer seems to be one of the most basic practices of Christianity. We pray in church. We pray in the privacy of our own rooms. We pray as we walk. We pray as we drive. Most often, we pray when we feel afraid or threatened, when we want to possess something, or when we want some condition to turn out our way. We pray before we eat. We pray also when we're thankful or joyful, but I suspect most would admit that we sometimes are not as vigilant in our prayers of thanksgiving.

The teachings of our churches affirm the New Testament message of Matthew, wherein the Apostles of Jesus asked, "Lord, how should we pray?" And Jesus gave them the words we call *The Lord's Prayer*. It has become my certain understanding that the prayer Jesus gave us is an affirmation of security and confidence, underscored by praise and thanksgiving. Yet, it seems most often to be repeated by rote as a prayer of supplication, sandwiched between beginning and ending declarations of praise. There is such a wealth of spiritual insight about The Lord's Prayer that faith leaders could impart to their followers. Some have. Far too many, though, steeped in traditional consciousness, have not themselves seen or heard the beautiful possibilities Jesus was suggesting in his template for perfect prayer. Stanza by stanza, these are insights I have gained through many years of faithful repetition and contemplation of The Lord's Prayer.

Our Father who art in heaven, hallowed be thy name.

That certainly appears to be a straightforward statement of praise and identification. It addresses God as Father, but we discussed gender possibilities in a previous chapter. It also declares the sanctity of God's name. There is, however, the matter of location. Jesus addresses, "Our Father…in heaven." My experience of the traditional teaching of the Christian church is, as I have already suggested, that heaven is a place—someplace out there, separate and apart from us. Having come to understand, however, heaven is a state of being more than a place of being, it is now clear to me that when I pray to God I must go within, as Jesus taught. My ability to access God, my inherent divinity, may depend upon the degree to which I have welcomed and nurtured heaven within my own spiritual heart, my divine consciousness, the degree to which I have released the force of resistance that is part and parcel of the ego. I believe there is also great significance in *hallowed be thy name*. If God's true name is I AM, and if I AM is also descriptive of our personal Divine nature, then we have a responsibility to respect ourselves, and others. Whether it's the thoughts we form, the words with which we express ourselves, the way we treat others, the things we put into our bodies, or the way we use and abuse our bodies and our minds. If each of us is the *Temple of the Most High*, mystically united with the Father/Mother God, it begs the question, "Do we fail to respect God when we disrespect another person, or ourselves?" Does such disrespect nullify the truth and power of *hallowed be thy name*?

Thy kingdom come, Thy will be done on Earth as it is in heaven.

For most of my life, this was, for me, a supplication. It was as though Jesus was saying, "Let Thy kingdom come," and, "Let Thy will be done on Earth as it is in heaven." I suspect the same is true for many others. I don't recall ever having been taught it was supplication, but I also don't recall ever having been taught it was an affirmation, as I now understand it to be. It is so very clear to me now, Jesus was declaring, "Thy kingdom is here, now, and Thy will is accomplished on Earth in and for those whose consciousness is heaven." Jesus taught us the kingdom of heaven is where and when we are, and we need only choose to enter in. It is the *Eternal Now*, obscured by the illusions of ego and the false reality we have built for ourselves in that Earth-based deception. I now ask myself, if God is God, how can God's own will not be done on Earth as it is in heaven? To suggest otherwise is to deny God is everywhere present and all-powerful. Among all that God is, much of which is indefinable by our current consciousness, God is unquestionably the Great Positive in all of creation. Jesus was surely making a positive affirmation of God's omniscience and omnipotence, and a declaration of the dimension of peace and joy that is available to us at all times, in every circumstance.

Give us this day our daily bread.

Again, I believe this is most often prayed as a supplication: "Please, God, give us this day our daily bread, please, please, please!" But, if God is total good and is the infinite and eternal Source, how could it not be God's will to give us every day our daily bread? I believe this is another positive affirmation. Jesus was saying, in a spirit of thanksgiving, "You give us always our daily bread." That some among us don't have enough to eat, and many in our world die of starvation each and every day is no argument that it is not God's will to feed all His children all the time. Rather, it is a condition of a divinely ordered world that is flawed by negative manifestations of human ego. God created a perfect world, but human ego recreated God, and thereby created less than perfect attitudes and experiences of life.

…and, forgive us our trespasses as we forgive those who trespass against us.

The first part of this phrase sounds like another plea for God's goodness, as though Jesus is saying, "Please forgive us our trespasses." If, however, God is love greater than we can fathom, how can there be any question of forgiveness? My relationship with Jesus causes me to know this is another affirmation, where He either said, or thankfully implied, "You forgive us our trespasses…" However, the second half of the declaration puts a different twist on it. "You forgive us our trespasses *as* we forgive those who trespass against us." In other words, we are forgiven according to the measure by which we forgive. It aligns itself with another place in scripture where Jesus is to have said "You receive according to the measure with which you give." That was a big *Aha!* for me, as one who has known a lifelong struggle, learning to forgive.

Yet, we cannot truly embrace and internalize the messages of Jesus without knowing that what we do to and for others, we also do to and for ourselves. Is this not just another demonstration of the action of cause and effect, Newton's Law? Jesus is teaching that whatever we sow we will also reap. Forgiveness and un-forgiveness flow through the same gateway. Though it is God's nature to always forgive us, we block that forgiveness by closing the gate that holds un-forgiveness within our own hearts. To carry the premise one step farther, when we ask God's forgiveness, yet refuse to forgive ourselves, we place our ego-selves above God, and cut ourselves off from the forgiveness we seek.

There is perhaps another dimension that might also be considered. Forgiveness is a response to judgment. Jesus was emphatic about our responsibility to refrain from judgment: "Judge not, that you be not also judged." In the absence of judgment, where is the need for forgiveness?

Lead us not into temptation, but deliver us from evil...

The only way I can possibly find authenticity in this statement is to hear it as an affirmation. Surely, Jesus actually said, or meant, "*You* lead us not into temptation..." It troubles me to consider how many Christians have prayed this, like I, never thinking or questioning, as though asking God not to lead us (me) into temptation. It does seem a bit of an oxymoron. After all, how could or would God possibly lead us into temptation? It is as contrary to God's nature as it is for pigs to fly. By the same standard, it must surely be God's nature always to deliver us from evil. There is varying thought among Christian thinkers as to what is meant by evil. Personally, I believe it probably refers to times or circumstances that trouble us, try us, or are a manifestation of personal or collective negativity. Time and again I have heard it said, and have said myself, that God is trying me. But, if God is all knowing and loving, what need or purpose could He possibly have in giving us trials? We simply live in a world and a state of common consciousness where trials are created by the action of our ego. It is always God's will to deliver us from those trials. That we don't always experience deliverance may be due to our own choices, or any number of circumstances relating to the free will and choice of others, but never because deliverance is not God's will.

For Thine is the kingdom, the power, and the glory forever.
These words were actually not part of the prayer of Jesus recorded in the original canon of the Christian church. It was added at the time of the Protestant Reformation, and disputed by the Catholic Church. There is certainly no misunderstanding or dispute, however, about this beautiful declaration of praise, and recognition of the vastness, greatness and glory of God.

Amen! And, Amen.

* * *

The Lord's Prayer, when prayed in consciousness that frees it from the limitations of Biblical print and ecclesiastical dogma, offers a whole new dimension, and a far richer example for us to follow in our personal prayer life. Here are some ways it has helped me to reform the nature of my own prayer experience.

I have come to understand that God, by God's nature, can only want what is good for me and can only offer me safety, joy and abundance. That such has not always been my experience says nothing about the nature and will of God. If sacred scripture owns any credibility, after all, it is most specific that we are given free will and that we live in a world of circumstances—a place where the sun shines on both the righteous and the unrighteous and storms descend upon all, without discrimination. Again, I am reminded of Rev. Pearl Kerwin who always said, "God is no respecter of persons." Jesus was not ambivalent about the power of thought and the spoken word, as we shall examine more carefully in the next chapter. For the moment, I would simply suggest the circumstances of our lives might not necessarily be the proverbial *will of God*, but largely the result of personal and collective consciousness and the actions derived from that consciousness. I have often referred to the lyrics of a song that gained significant popularity more than twenty years ago: "I beg your pardon/I never promised you a rose garden." I like to say God wrote that. In truth God did, for it was written by a human among us, songwriter Joe South, *God's only begotten son.* As I read the scriptures and listen meditatively to Spirit, no rose garden was ever promised. The promise was that, "I will be with you, wherever you go and whatever the world hands you. I will be your fortress and your comforter (paraphrased)." When we divorce ourselves from the belief that everything that happens to us is God's will, and own our personal responsibility for the circumstances of our life, mystical and intangible as that may sometimes be, how can our prayer be anything but praise and thanksgiving for God who unceasingly offers us protection and victory? How can it not be an affirmation of our will to demonstrate all the good that is ours to give and receive?

The affirmation part is one of the places where I believe the Christian church has most failed us. In teaching us to pray from a consciousness of lack, i.e. begging, supplication, declarations of want or need, many leaders have turned our minds to negativity, often delving into attitudes of fear. Just as darkness is nothing more than the absence of light, fear is the absence of love, and scripture clearly declares that, "God is love, and all who abide in love, abide in God, and God in them." If God is Divine Spirit, totally good, totally positive, and totally impartial, then we do well to ask ourselves whether we can even access God through negative consciousness. It may be like praying for light in a darkened room when we have failed to turn on the switch. The scriptural teachings attributed to Jesus give us wonderful assurances. "It is the Father's good pleasure to give you all that you ask." "Whatsoever you ask in faith, believing, it shall be done for you." "If you had faith even the size of a mustard seed you would say to this mountain, 'Move,' and it would be moved." "What father among you, if his child asked for a fish, would give him a serpent, or if he asked for a loaf of bread, would give him a stone? How much greater is the love the heavenly Father has for you?" Yet, when we pray from a consciousness of negativity, fearing or lacking, I have come to understand that we block the flow of good—the channels through which the love of God blesses us. Jesus told us to pray knowing that we have already received, and that such faith will produce the results we want. I have found the diligent and repeated use of positive affirmations to be one of the most important and accessible prayer tools available to me in re-forming my consciousness from negative to positive. It has helped me to become a *possibility* thinker. My experience has shown me it is the possibility thinkers who become the receivers and the doers, regardless of their faith, or lack thereof.

Earlier, I suggested God is, among other things, Divine Law, law that is immutable, non-discriminating, and non-failing. If what we ask for, then, is good, and if our faith is the kind of believing that is *knowing*, we can rest assured what we ask for will come to us in Divine timing—that, or something better. Where we often get hung up is in our own impatience. We want everything to occur according to our time line—Earth time. There is, however, no such thing as time in Spirit, the eternal now, in which every moment is the present moment. When our good doesn't arrive according to our own schedule we often become doubtful or discouraged, and that sends a negative signal to Spirit, which always responds according to the signals we send. Our doubt causes detours and roadblocks that delay, and sometimes abort, the delivery of our good. I'm at this moment reminded of Gloria and Bill Gaither's beautiful gospel hymn, "I Believe, Help Thou My Unbelief."

Steeped in the daily discipline of prayer, it was that same activity that was one of the most influential factors causing me to question traditional Christianity. Prayer was always a practice of talking to God—praising him, and telling him a whole laundry list of fears and petitions. Having been raised in fundamentalism from birth, I was very adept, and onlookers were often amazed at the eloquence and comfort with which I could address God aloud in the midst of any group or worship scenario. I could perform as well as any of the televangelists, and it was sincere, as I hope they are. At some point, though, I began to question the need to tell God anything. If I truly believed God is Omniscient, what could I possibly tell him He does not already know? My work and associations had introduced me to some of the practices of people of other traditions and I slowly began to realize the power that exists in listening—allowing God to talk to me. "Be still," the scripture says, "and know that I AM God." It became clear the people of the eastern religions who meditate and the Christian mystics who meditate, are simply listening—creating a void within themselves where they can hear and know. I began far too late in life to develop a daily discipline of meditation the first thing each morning, and it made more difference for me than I can tell.

An added dimension of meditation, opened up for me by new thought teachers whose works I began to devour during my process of separation, is visualization. If I sit quietly, clearing my mind of every-thing but the good and positive I want for my life, then create a picture in my mind and focus passionately upon that visualization, my divine power of co-creation, promised to me by Jesus, my Lord, proves itself in desired expressions of manifestation. A recent, profound example oc-curred several months ago when I required a rather radical surgery that is famous for negative side effects and difficult recovery. I determined that I would be an exception to the rule, and I set that intention so firmly in my consciousness that I could see it no other way. Whenever doubt or fear began to creep into my thought processes I immediately banished it and replaced it with positive affirmations. During my daily meditation I envisioned myself swiftly and fully recovered, without difficult or negative manifestations. So it was. The nurses who cared for me in the hospital could not believe how swiftly and comfortably I improved while in their care, and my physicians were thrilled. Within five weeks I was back on my bicycle.

I have a son of very high spiritual consciousness who has two daugh-ters still in the wonderful years of childhood. He and my daughter-in-law are teaching those two most fortunate little girls the tools of creation—how to use them for the manifestation of good. What blessed children! How much more joyful would have been the quality of my own journey, had I learned as a child to incorporate into my prayer life those activities that could have created for me the reality that I truly wanted?

I am reminded of one Palm Sunday in the middle 1990s when,

having not been regular attendants of the Sunday Mass for quite some time, my wife and I went to the biggest and most prestigious Catholic Church in Reno. When it came time for the *Prayers of the Faithful*, the priest celebrant said with enthusiasm, "Now, everybody pray real loud so God can hear you." I could hardly contain myself from standing up and screaming, "Oh, for God's sake, get a clue." He was sincere, though, and had no understanding that the God to which he was praying dwelt within him, and within every member of that congregation. I was, again, called to bless him on his journey of faith, as I expect others to do for me.

There are countless best-selling books and testimonials of motivational speakers who have experienced for themselves the truth of Jesus that the prayer of the believer always produces the desired results. I believe that were Jesus to speak to us in a language compatible with contemporary culture and consciousness, he would say it like this. "Because each and every human person is the indwelling Presence of God, the one who fully believes in his or her personal divinity always manifests the results of his or her deliberate intentions." It makes no difference whether we call the energy that serves our homes electricity, juice, or fire. If we are connected to it, and access it in divinely (scientifically) ordered ways, it still runs the fridge. It's according to the lyrics, by Johnny Mercer, of the big band era hit, "You've got to accentuate the positive/ Eliminate all the negative/Latch on to the affirmative/Don't mess with Mr. In Between." Through my life experience and spiritual work with countless others, I have come to understand a powerful truth not taught by traditional Christianity. If God is the substance of all, expressing in all and through all, then all who work within the framework of Divine Law will realize the desired results—the manifestation of their good. What a fitting segue to reflections on Co-Creativity.

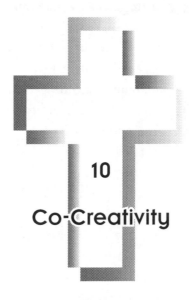

10

Co-Creativity

First, God created the world; then, God created humankind. Thereafter, humankind created a mess. For many years I believed the condition of this world and the circumstances of my life were the will of God. Now, I can only ask, could starvation, war, genocide and unimaginable cruelty possibly be the will of a God of Infinite Love? Do we not blaspheme when we suggest that any circumstance that does not convey peace, love, joy and abundance is part of the Divine plan and will of the God of peace, love, joy and abundance? Yet, from my earliest childhood and even to the present day I have heard Christians, leaders and followers, declare acceptance of and resignation to destructive or unhappy conditions in their personal lives, and in the world. "If it is God's will that I have cancer, I can accept it." "God took my child because He needed another angel for his heaven." "AIDS is God's judgment upon homosexuals." "God is testing my faith" or, "God is testing your faith by the severity of your circumstance," as if an all-knowing God ever needed to test anything or anybody.

Jesus was not casual about our personal power, and our responsibility to use it only for good. Throughout his documented ministry there were exhortations and admonishments surrounding the creative power of both word and thought. "All that I have done, you can do too." "Do your scriptures not say 'You are gods'?" "Speak but the word, and it will be done for you." "As a man thinks, he will become." "Where your treasure lies, your heart will be also." "Seek, and you shall find; knock, and the door will be opened; ask, and it shall be given." When he performed his healing miracles, he adamantly encouraged his subjects to accept their own responsibility, and change the conditions of their lives. "Pick up your bed and walk." "Go, and sin no more," (go and change your consciousness). "Your faith has made you whole," (your consciousness has corrected the circumstances of your life.)

Once I abandoned the concept of a deity that was *out there*, and I began to understand what Jesus meant when he said, "…go to the Father within," and, "When you pray, go into your closet…" (go within), I realized the Divine Presence is actually manifest in every cell, every atom, of my total being. It was then I began to understand my inherent power, responsibility and potential as a co-creator with God. The teachings of Jesus became increasingly clear to me; the basic tools of creation are thought and the spoken word. They are the implements with which we apply the incredible, divine power that lies within us to create, destroy, and recreate the circumstances of our lives, our personal reality. That my life may not fully reflect what I want or wanted simply affirms my past ignorance of the power that is mine, and my failure to use the tools responsibly. In my garage I have an electric skill saw with which I have cut lumber for various home improvements. Used properly, the pieces I cut fit together perfectly, and the final result is just as I envisioned it to be. Used sloppily, my finished product is not one of which I can be proud. Once when I was careless, the power tool ripped through my denim trousers and barely missed making a very serious cut into my leg at a spot where my femoral aortic artery could have been severed. More than once I have carelessly cut the power cord, leaving the marvelous tool completely inoperable. I find these to be analogies similar to the power, both constructive and destructive, that exists for all of us in our use of thought and the spoken word.

Most of us have seen magazine advertisements for the metaphysical philosophy of the Rosicrucians, that declares, "Thoughts are things," I personally believe Jesus made that assertion emphatically clear. In so many of his teachings he either stated or implied the creative power of thought and its ability to impact objects and persons. Many will remember the entertainer Uri Geller who used to appear on television variety shows in the 1950s and 1960s. One of Mr. Geller's most remarkable feats was to concentrate intensely upon a spoon or fork, while the audience watched it curl and twist before their eyes. He would also move objects with just the power of his mind. And, who has not felt someone staring at them, and turned quickly to meet the eyes of one whose attention was focused directly upon them? Conversely, how many times have you stared intently at someone and had that person turn around and look back at you?

Ernest Holmes, the previously mentioned explorer in new thought philosophies and founder of the Church of Religious Science, said, following the teachings of the Master, "Where attention goes, energy flows." Energy is our power, the God presence within us. The more we focus our attention upon a thought, a subject, a purpose, an intention, the more energy flows to it, and creativity is set into motion. Opening my mind to universal wisdom has caused me to understand that when we honestly consider how we use our energy, where we have focused it and where we have scattered it, we can hardly wonder why our lives contain circumstances we'd rather not have.

Overcoming fear to examine philosophies outside the restrictive limits of traditional Christian dogma has given me critical and essential, experiential understanding of the previously discussed *Law of Attraction*—"that which is like unto itself is drawn." Our thoughts, our words, and our behaviors are magnets that attract to us more of whatever it is we are generating from the vibration of our personal consciousness.

I have a friend of many years, a devout Christian lady who is active in her church, and who can quote the BIBLE as quickly and accurately as though she wrote it. Ruby (a fictitious name) is one of the most negative thinkers I have ever known. She seems to focus an inordinate amount of thought on the subversive activities of *the evil one*. Most anything bad that can possibly happen to her does. It is just one disaster or disappointment after another, from health issues, to family trouble, to

financial distress, to mechanical problems, to trouble with neighbors—
you name it. The list goes on and on endlessly, not just for a short period
of time, but for years. Though she claims the Power of God and the
mastership of Jesus, she constantly affirms that she is under attack from
the evil one. Consequently, she seems always to get what she names. I so
often want to say, "Ruby, don't you know that you're your own worst
enemy? The Lord you believe in taught you that your thoughts and your
words are powerful creators, but you have not heard it. You continue to
use those magnificent tools of creation to bring to yourself all that you
don't want." Sadly, her consciousness is such that she would not hear it,
and such a suggestion from me would likely alienate her. I have learned
the hard way that everyone is entitled to their own pathway and pace on
the journey to enlightenment. If they're not asking the question, they're
not likely to want to hear the answer. The job of one who would teach
is often to simply be a patient and silent example.

During the latter years of my professional life in spiritual healthcare,
I became most interested in the use of prayer energy to affect positive
outcomes during surgery. Among the first in western healthcare to in-
tegrate chaplains into surgical teams, I was privileged to observe some
fairly astounding outcomes. During that period, one of my chaplains
had a twelve-year old son who lived with congenital heart defects.
Hoping to improve the quality of his life, Richie and his parents agreed
to a proposed ablation whereby the heart surgeon would use an electronic scalpel to open a new channel between the atrium and ventricle,
two major chambers of his heart. The procedure was not without risk,
so Richie had requested that I be in the operating room to prayerfully
facilitate energy management during the surgery. Because Richie was
hospitalized in another city, and at an institution where I did not have
privileges, I was denied presence in the surgical suite. However, the staff
was most gracious to make me comfortable in a nearby room where I
could do my energy work in conjunction with the activities of the surgical team. Each time the family received a progress report from inside
the surgical suite, Richie's father gave me a report.

It was that day I learned most profoundly the power of prayer energy, and the importance of being specific about your intentions during

prayer work. Having failed to understand the true nature and purpose of the surgery, I had for the first hour and a half worked against the goal of the surgical team. I thought they were working only with one chamber, striving to keep the laser from burning through the muscle into the other. I had put myself into a meditative state and was intently focused upon Richie's heart, envisioning the muscle giving unyielding resistance to the laser scalpel. About an hour and a half into the procedure his father came to report to me that Richie was holding up well, and everything seemed to be going successfully, except that the surgeon seemed unable to burn the desired channel opening. The laser was turned on to full intensity, but the muscle would not give way to the new channel. "OMIGOD," I thought. I'm working against them." Without betraying myself to Richie's father, I went immediately back to prayer, envisioning a perfect channel opening at the demand of the laser scalpel. Within a very short time Richie's father returned to tell me that the surgery was completed successfully and Richie was doing great.

Words, too, are powerful, creative tools. "Speak the word," the Master said, "and it shall be done for you." The whole creation chronicle in the first chapter of Genesis, though I know it to be analogy, bespeaks the creative power of the spoken word. Word, of course, is a progression and physical communication of thought. The two are cooperative tools with which we are co-creators with God.

Words are self-fulfilling. They might be compared to building blocks. If a mason lays just one block upon a foundation, it is no obstacle to anyone. If he lays several more in the same spot, it is still possible to see over them, or navigate around them. If he continues to lay those blocks, however, he eventually creates a wall or structure over which he may not be able to see, and which may present an obstacle to his progress.

Consider how often you have known persons to express thoughts or attitudes repeatedly in negative ways until the thing of which they spoke, possibly even feared became their reality. Throughout many of my younger years I was known to jokingly exclaim, "When my ship comes in the dock will probably be on strike!" If my ship ever did come in during that time, the dock would surely be on strike, because I received little of the precious cargo which I so desired. Many years have been spent taking down that wall, and I know one thing for certain. Taking down a haphazardly built wall is far more difficult than creating a beautiful pathway.

I've known more than one person who was often heard to say "I'll probably die young." To the sorrow of those who loved them, that is exactly what they did. There is a case for understanding that a seemingly untimely death was something in their destiny that they personally intuited. The case is as strong, though, that they created the event by misuse of thought and word.

I remember a young woman I counseled many years ago. One evening during her teen years she ingested too much of a certain street substance, and gave her body to a group of anxious boys, one after the other. Raised in a devout Christian home, her guilt and self-judgment was unrelenting. I cannot begin to count the occasions I heard her sob that she deserved to die. She should have breast cancer. Self-condemnation was so ingrained that she could never be lifted to a consciousness that enabled her to release the past. Sadly, she died of breast cancer before she was forty years old. What a perfect example of the many persons I have known who lived in negative consciousness, whether fear or the lack of forgiveness, continually forming words that bespoke that consciousness, for whom it became their eventual reality.

How the Christian church has failed us, I have come to believe, in dogmatizing our beautiful, divine- power of co-creativity with God rather than teaching us how to claim it, and use it responsibly!

I AM

If God's most Holy Name is I AM, and God is the fiber of our very being, atom for atom, as I have come to understand the teaching of Jesus, my name and your name must also be I AM. Whenever I take God's name in vain, I misuse my own—I disrespect myself. How I wish I had a dollar for every time I have formed negative thoughts, or made limiting, destructive statements such as I am sad, I am broke, I am tired,

I am sick, I am frustrated, I am angry, I am hungry, I am stuck, I am afraid, I am unlucky, etc. I have come to understand that every time I use the sacred name I AM, I affirm and strengthen a condition that has already manifested for me, or I create the *embryo* of a condition that corresponds to my thought or word.

"For every action, there is an equal and opposite reaction." Every thought we form and every word we speak goes forth into the ethers, the undivided Divine Presence, and a reaction occurs, even as a stone tossed into a quiet pond sends rings of water outward from the point of impact. I AM now increasingly mindful to use God's sacred name, my mystical, personal identity, only in ways that create or affirm the conditions and circumstances I want for my life. Certainly, I cannot deny feelings or appearances that may be less than I desire. However, as I grow in spiritual consciousness I become more mindful to cautiously name them for what they are, feelings or appearances, rather than to misuse my creative energy by affirming them as reality. "I feel sick right now," or "I currently appear to be short of money," is a less permanent and more spiritually responsible way of describing an experience or appearance that is not what I want.

At first, taking charge of the manner in which I use my personal I AM was akin to a trick my grandfather taught me as a very young child. He assured me that the way to catch a wild bird is to sprinkle salt on its tail. Somehow, those elusive birds never sat still long enough for me to approach them with a saltshaker. So it is with the two words I have been accustomed to using automatically, without any forethought, for my entire life. However, conscious intention always bears desired results. I now realize increasing control over the manner in which I dispense my I AM to the universe, and when I catch myself using it negatively I quickly delete the thought or words just as I might hit the delete key on my computer. A statement as simple as, "Cancel, cancel," seems to work fine. Then I can reform my thought and re-apply my personal I AM more responsibly. Because feeling is a critical component of creativity I am deliberate about creating a level of feeling that resonates with the desired intention.

I once attended a motivational seminar where the keynote speaker was a delightful woman whose name I no longer remember. In emphasizing the *power of positive thinking*, she stated that whenever anyone asked her how she was, her standard response was, "I'm just super-fine and getting better." Realizing that was a very creative application of the wisdom of Jesus, I decided to give it a try. Many were the times, during the remaining years of my professional life, when passing fellow employees in the hallways of hospitals where I worked, I heard them automatically say "How are you?" or, "How's it going?" My standard response became, "I'm super-fine and getting better." I soon began to observe that no matter what kind of burden I might be carrying, I felt better by making such a positive declaration. I consider it a beautiful demonstration of the creative power of thought and the spoken word to affect appearances and outcomes.

Turning the sacred name around, how often in our daily lives do we declare to another, "You are…?" You are so smart. You are so beautiful. You are stupid. You are a failure. You are disgusting. You are a witch (I never could spell). I believe Jesus was calling our attention just as profoundly to the creative power of such declarations. When another person has a particular perception of self, whether positive or negative, and we affirm it with our own thought or word, we increase the Divine Force that makes it so. If one has within self an *unplanted field*, and a mind receptive to the suggestion of others, our thoughts or words can be seeds that produce results akin to their own likeness. How I wish that such had been my understanding when my children were in their formative years, for I now see more than ever the extreme and sacred responsibility adults have to the children in their care, whether they are parents, grandparents, aunts, uncles, teachers, neighbors or spiritual leaders. Our responsibility to others, especially the weak and vulnerable, in the way we use our Divine Power of creativity is incomprehensible, and the way we demonstrate that responsibility can be Earth shattering.

"Everything old is new again," proclaimed the theme song from the musical production *Thoroughly Modern Millie*. Jesus was surely, in his own time, *New Age*, and judged by most with contempt for the extraordinary things he taught about God and the meaning of life. His consciousness and his teachings were simply beyond the dogma and understanding of the day, and for that he was nailed to a cross. His consciousness has re-emerged in our own time in ways beyond the collective dogma of the Christian church, and it is as vehemently denied and condemned by those who cannot or will not see, even though *New Thought* is no longer punishable by death—not, at least, in Christian cultures. Historically, however, institutional Christianity has not looked kindly upon those who dared to think *outside the box*, or explore possibilities that were not in keeping with the party line.

How different would have been the quality of my life—and that of the many people whose lives have been influenced by my ministry—if the churches in which my trust was placed had taught, perhaps even understood, the *truth* of Jesus that thoughts and words are forces of unfathomable creative power? Indeed, if we place any credibility at all in the red-letter teachings of Jesus, we cannot deny the power of thought and word to create and to influence. We need only, if we are honest, to examine our own lives to see the power with which the thought patterns upon which we dwell and the words we speak have influenced our lives and formed our own reality.

I had a very beloved family member, a devout, Christian lady of a fundamentalist denomination, who seemed always to expect the worst of things. One day when a neighbor asked her how she was feeling, she replied, "Well, I'm just fine today, but then you never know how I'll be tomorrow." To expect to be well was a bit of a stretch for her imagination, and her expectations were rarely disappointed.

Another family member has always projected an upbeat, positive attitude. In her advancing years, however, her thoughts and words most often reflect negativity. Nothing ever seems to be totally right. It's always, "Yes, but..." No matter how happy or promising the situation she describes, there is always something that didn't go right, or that might go wrong. Nothing in her life, or the lives of those she loves, ever seems to be quite as she would have it to be. She has projected that state of mind for so long it has become self-fulfilling. Even the best circumstances and experiences of her life seem always to have some difficult or unpleasant aspect. She has no understanding of her personal responsibility as a creator of outcomes that are less than she desires, nor is she willing to reform the attitude that so profoundly skews her creative process.

By contrast, I am reminded of the mother of a ling-time friend. Though not overtly religious, Dorothy was a woman of faith consciousness, and one of the most positive minded persons I have ever known. If she ever had negative things to say about anyone or anything, I never heard it. She was always positive and upbeat, whatever the circumstances of her life. Certainly, she had challenges and disappointments, but if anyone asked her how things were for her, they were always "Just fine." Likewise, she was just fine. She was a happy soul who spread happiness to those around her.

It's interesting to observe the way in which so many Divine truths seem to play out in the music of every age. I recall a song made popular some years ago by Frank Sinatra, "High Hopes," and it dealt with the ability to accomplish anything you *think* you can accomplish. And, again, Jesus said, "As you think in your heart, so it shall be for you." "If your faith is as great as a mustard seed…" As already discussed, that is the kind of faith that is *knowing*. Such faith, however, is the product of a vast amalgamation of thought, introspection and experience.

There are well proven religious practices in the world whereby the power of intention—thought—is used negatively for the accomplishment of destruction. Probably the most familiar to western hemisphere Christians are Voodoo and Satanism—stellar examples of the misuse of the I AM. Such practices might present a bit of a conundrum for one such as I who has come to disavow the existence of Satan, or any evil force at enmity with God, were it not for my realization of the true nature of God, as I believe I have been taught by my Lord. *God is Spirit.*

If the supremely intelligent Divine Energy which is both Creator and created, everywhere present, is by its very nature accessible to all who use it, regardless of their religion or faith practice, then it must surely be accessible to those who would use it for bad, as well as those who would use it for good. That in no way negates the truth that God is inherently and only good. It does suggest, however, that those so steeped in the consciousness of duality they have placed their faith in the dark side—negativity—are able to use the wonderful divine energy in ways that are not for good. As stated already in several previous chapters, electricity, the force that does so many good and creative things for us, also has power for destruction if not used responsibly. Divine Spirit, the Infinite, eternal Father/Mother Creator, God, as it were, cannot operate any way except according to His/Her/Its own nature—irrevocable, immutable Divine Law without judgment or bias for individual persons. Good though *She* is, *He* can be used for bad results without in any way negating the fact of *Its* inherent purity of purpose.

This understanding solves for us the question of spiritual warfare and of any powerful being at enmity with God. All is reduced to the true nature of God, to our personal responsibility for using our own I AM, respectfully, and only according to Divine nature—*good*. It also reflects the *duality* consciousness from which we all endure repeated lifetimes on planet Earth as we struggle fitfully to awaken from the dream of separation—ego verses divinity. Traditional Christian thought calls Jesus the, "only begotten Son of God." I believe however, if God is One, All, and Undivided, then all are the *only begotten*. For more than 2,000 years, Jesus has sounded the alarm to awaken us, yet we slumber on.

Mother Theresa of Calcutta was one who *got it*. Steeped as she was in Catholicism, and obedient to the dogma of her faith, her words and her example spoke a profound consciousness of the Divine Presence within herself, and in every human person. Yet, her diaries and the writings published since her death attest the doubt and uncertainty with which she sometimes struggled, much akin to the cry of Jesus from the cross, "My God, my God, why have you forsaken me?" Ego consciousness, difficult as it is to abandon, is not a force at enmity with God. Rather, it is a *cloud of unknowing*, a sometimes glorious and sometimes ghastly illusion that belongs only to this Earth-plane of life. Our role is to find our way through the fog, and into the Light. Again, Jesus said, "The kingdom of heaven is now. Enter in."

11

Miracles

There's no such thing as a miracle. WOW! That got your attention, didn't it? Where's this crackpot coming from? The scriptures are replete with beautiful, hope-filled accounts of the miracles of Jesus. He healed the blind men, the lepers, the lame, and the woman with the relentless issue of blood. He multiplied the loaves and fishes, raised the dead, and turned water into wine at the wedding feast of Cana, all of which was trumped by his greatest feat of all, resurrection from the dead. Are we to abandon faith in all those awesome examples of the Divinity of Jesus? Not for my part. They are integral to the foundation of my relationship with my Lord and I believe them profoundly. I also believe Him when He said "All that I have done, you can do too; and greater far…" Were we sitting on a grassy hillside today, listening to Jesus teach in a manner compatible with 21st century consciousness, I believe He would say to us that the things we believe to be miracles are really just the natural order— Divine Order, so to speak. We just don't understand our minds have the power to affect and alter atoms and their pre-determined patterns. However profoundly we may proclaim we are created in the image and likeness of God, or any among us may declare, as Jesus taught, we are manifestations of the Divine, with power to do all things, our realization and utilization of that incredible identity is, at best, minimal, sporadic and fleeting.

As a young man during the 1960s, I often watched a weekly television show called *I Believe in Miracles*, produced by the late, Christian evangelist, Kathryn Kuhlman. Though controversial, as are most such ministers of healing, and sometimes even comical, I chanced to be personally acquainted with several persons who attended her huge healing services in Los Angeles, and I was closely associated with one woman who experienced healing through Kathryn Kuhlman's intervention. I believe her to have been a sincere, if sometimes imperfect, minister of God, and a lover of the Lord in whose name she worked. Kathryn always began her services with this very dramatic and profound exhortation: "I believe in miracles—because—I believe in God!" One could scarcely discount her personal conviction in that declaration. She did believe in miracles. I wonder how much more authentic her ministry might have been had she been so conscious as to have declared, "I believe miracles are expressions of Divine Order, and are the birthright of each and every one of God's children."

During my years as a spiritual health care provider, I witnessed, was even party to, many seemingly miraculous things. I remember the time when an elderly Native American gentleman, a citizen of a nearby Reservation, spent many weeks languishing in the Intensive Care Unit of the hospital where I was employed. When all medical hope was exhausted, the physicians met with his wife, a wizened little woman who appeared to be a hold-over from the nineteenth century, and told her it was time to remove all mechanical life support from her husband and let him go. She would not hear of it until a particular medicine man had come from another Reservation nearly 2,000 miles away. The doctors treated her compassionately, and agreed to continue their extraordinary care of her husband until her shaman could come. The wait was nearly two weeks.

How well I recall the day he arrived. Because the ICU did not have independent rooms, patient beds were separated only by drapes that could be opened or closed. We were all on pins and needles in expectation of the chanting and dancing that might occur around the patient's bed. Nonetheless, we determined to respect the faith practices of our patient and his family, and the shaman showed respect for other patients by working quietly, reverently and mysteriously. Within a very short time after his departure, our patient began to show signs of improvement. I don't recall whether the recovery was a matter of days or weeks. I only remember, to the amazement of the entire medical staff, the old man walked out of our hospital and went home to his people. Was it a miracle? At the time I thought so. Now, I believe it was natural order. The Shaman was so in touch with the Spirit of God within him, his own divinity, he was able to interact with the divinity resident in the patient. That which was divided by ego consciousness became once again united. To state it in less religious terms, there are controlled, laboratory studies indicating if a person, place or thing has a stronger vibration than other persons, places or things in its environment, it will influence the weaker vibrations to come into alignment with its vibration. The stronger vibration wins.

On another occasion, while working in the same hospital, I prayed one evening with a very frightened man who was to have surgery the following morning for removal of a malignant tumor on his liver. The patient was a Catholic man who had not been particularly conscientious about the practice of his faith. I placed my hands upon his body and prayed after the manner in which I often did, feeling compassion and hope for him, but I recall no lightning bolts or choirs of angels. However, during pre-surgical preparations on the following morning it was determined there had been a significant change in his condition. Ensuing studies revealed the tumor known to be there on the previous day was totally gone. The surgery was cancelled, and the patient went home. Was it a miracle? I thought so then, but not so now.

I once lived in a small community where a child with Downs-Syndrome was being raised by her grandfather, and her wheelchair bound grandmother who had not stood on her own or walked for years. One day the child was playing in the front yard of her home, watched by her grandmother who sat in her wheelchair near the sidewalk that separated the yard from a busy street. Just as a speeding car rounded the adjacent curve, the child strayed into the street. Her grandmother sprang out of the wheelchair, ran to the child in time to pull her free from the oncoming car, and then collapsed back into the chair from which she still could not move without assistance. Was it a miracle? My faith at the time was certain of it. My present consciousness knows better.

As a young man, my knees were broken simultaneously when I was struck by a speeding car and thrown forty feet from the point of impact. During the years that followed, I often experienced pain and weakness in both knees, even though the fractures healed without any dislocation. Sixteen years after the injury I was participating in a charismatic prayer meeting at the Catholic parish to which I belonged. It was the cold of winter in the Pacific Northwest where I lived at the time, and I recall experiencing considerable discomfort in my knees that evening. When I asked for prayer, the group gathered around me and began singing and praying, each member in his or her personal prayer tongue. As many as could, laid hands upon my knees. When the praying had stopped, I became very aware the pain was gone. Leaving the meeting, my knees felt stronger and I was able to walk with confidence. Nearly twenty-five years passed before the process of aging caused me to again experience symptoms in those knees. Even now, the discomfort has never equaled that which I experienced before the spontaneous healing in that beautiful prayer meeting. Was it a miracle? To the contrary, it was divine—the ever present and always accessible power of love.

Virtually millions of people have traveled great distances to visit holy sites, so named for the miracles credited to them. Among them, the famed Cathedral of Our Lady of Guadalupe in Mexico City, and the waters of Lourdes in France are replete with plaques placed there as a testimony of thanksgiving from those who have experienced so-called miraculous healings as a result of their pilgrimage to that site; crutches and wheelchairs are often left by those who no longer need them. How does this happen? Is God one whose love discriminates among His children, finding favor with some, and disfavor with others whose needs may be even greater, those who may even live more righteously? Why would a God of love heal an aging person who may have lived a hardened life, and overlook an innocent child suffering major health challenges, even facing death? Why are there reputed holy sites around the world where people of non-Christian faith bear testimony to the same seemingly miraculous experiences?

Jesus is reported to specifically have said, "Your faith has made you whole." That faith, I have come to understand, is not a belief system, or a heart full of hope. It is conviction, knowing, a consciousness of Divine Presence and where to access it, a consciousness of Divine Law, and how to use it. Such faith is a personal willpower that frees itself from the hold of ego just long enough to experience unity with the Infinite and Eternal Source. I once knew a Christian Science practitioner who told me I would experience instant healing, if I could, even for a split second, free myself from the hold of ego so completely that I could know, as did Jesus, that "The Father and I are one." It was some years before I understood the consciousness to which she referred was what Jesus meant when he said, "Your faith has made you whole." Few, perhaps none, among us have the kind of faith that sustains us in the constant state of Divine expression Jesus knew so profoundly. Were it different, we would be free of the limitations of this world, constantly healing the sick, raising the dead, multiplying matter and demonstrating abundant good, as did Jesus, wherever we went. We would live in a state of Divine Order, heaven, here and now. At our best, we embrace the fullness of the divine only occasionally and briefly, if at all, and the Divinely Ordered results of those encounters are popularly called miracles.

I no longer believe in miracles. I do believe, however, in the Universal Presence of God, working in all, through all, and as all. I believe ALL things are possible to us when, often unknowing, our egos drop their guard long enough for the Divine flow to express. I know, like untold numbers of others, Christian and non-Christian, I have personally experienced or witnessed extraordinary things that were beyond the explanation of human logic, or science, as we know it. And again, Jesus said, "All things that I have done you can do too, and greater far." Separating such a powerful message from the shackles of traditional dogma and hearing its ageless truth according to a higher consciousness pushed me closer to the exit doors of traditional Christianity.

12

Sin

I remember with humorous fondness, a college acquaintance who was a great, great granddaughter of the famed Mormon pioneer Brigham Young. When Jan really felt like using a dirty expletive, she would say, "Oh, sin!" That seemed to be the most unholy thing she dared say. Of course, that was more socially acceptable than the profanity or toilet language I, or my fraternity brothers might have chosen. I believe her practice reflects the disdain with which sin has been held in Christian consciousness for 2,000 years, and in the minds of our Jewish forefathers before that.

Judeo-Christian history, as well as Islam, Hindu, and most major religions of the world, records cruel, often heinous, punishments meted out to *sinners* for an often unbelievable variety of abominations such as blasphemy, adultery, masturbation, marriage outside the *true* faith, varieties of disobedience, and expressing behaviors that in some Christian congregations might today be considered *Gifts of the Spirit*.

Throughout my years of official ministry, I have found it interesting to observe how many people never thought seriously about sin, except to avoid it where they could, or to beat themselves with guilt when they succumbed. Many things authority figures, including parents and the Christian church, have named as sinful, are most delicious, if in fact, wicked. I've listened to guilt ridden penitents cast off torturous burdens of sins which covered a broad spectrum from transgressions of any of the Ten Commandments, to social and moral laws evolved from Biblical times, to infractions of contemporary social mores, to the failure to keep various church laws governing diet, sexuality, fasting, tithing, and attendance at Sabbath worship. It is heart wrenching to recall the souls I have known who were unable to find self-forgiveness for sins of the past, and who were, therefore, unable to face impending death with peace, confidence and hope.

I cannot count the number of elderly women to whom I have ministered who, fearing judgment and eternal damnation, could not let go of this world because of an abortion they had held secret for sixty or seventy years. Their *sin* was often hidden in the days when such things were accomplished with a knitting needle, or a wire coat hanger.

I have cared for untold numbers struggling with chronic health conditions often categorized as psychosomatic, who, when they trusted me enough to bare their souls, revealed some sin, or amalgamation of sins, for which they had never forgiven themselves—sins for which they felt unworthy of God's forgiveness. How often their health condition seemed a perfect metaphor for punishment, or personal atonement for their sins.

Even today I know a man in his early 90s for whom life has lost its joy. A very moral, honest family man, respected by all in the small community where he has lived most of his life, and a lifelong practicing Catholic, he is obsessively conflicted because he longs for death but is terrified of God's judgment of his *sinful nature.* While most who know him might not imagine what those sins could possibly be, he alludes to a burden of guilt over youthful masturbation that religious educators assured him was vile and disgusting in the eyes of God.

In my walk with Jesus beyond the confines of Christianity, I came to understand there is no such thing as sin beyond the failure to love. Consider the Ten Commandments. An infraction of any one of them is, on the bottom line, a failure to love oneself, one's neighbor, or God. Jesus seemed to emphasize that when he said, "I give you a new commandment which is greater than all the rest. You shall love the Lord your God with your whole heart, and your neighbor as yourself." That commandment, perhaps, takes a lot of emphasis off trivial things which we have borne heavily in our hearts or carried to the confessional, and it places certain responsibility upon attitudes and social behaviors we may often have disregarded, or treated casually.

When my journey carried me to the consciousness of God as the infinitely good, Divine Energy of life that is present, without ceasing, throughout all of creation, I began to understand that failure to love either my neighbor or myself is always and without exception the failure to love God. Though the presentation and behavior of my neighbor's ego self may be unpalatable or unacceptable to me, whenever I fail to look beyond that illusion and see God who or which is present in all, I fail to love God. Whenever I fail to forgive my neighbor for the ways my ego self has felt judged, rejected or wounded by his or her ego self, I hold enmity toward God, which translates to enmity toward self. God is not and cannot be divided. Whatever I do to another, I do to myself, and vice-versa. After the same manner, I can beg God's forgiveness, relentlessly, yet not realize it when I fail to forgive myself. Failure to forgive self is an ego ploy that places self above God. Self-forgiveness, however, is the fullest realization of God's forgiveness.

What a tragedy that judgment is far too often taught by faith leaders in whom we place our trust. A contemporary example is Rev. Pat Robertson, the long-time televangelist from the 700 Club that is so popular among the political right wing, and the Evangelical sector of Christianity. In March, 2012, Rev. Robertson was queried by a woman conscientiously struggling because her sister, an admitted lesbian, was making plans to be married to another woman and had asked her to be a bridesmaid. The influential faith leader advised the woman that it was inappropriate for her to serve as a bridesmaid or even attend her lesbian sister's wedding to another woman. "If she doesn't like it, if she breaks off the union between you," was his counsel, "that's tough luck." He substantiated his wisdom with nebulous scriptures from the BIBLE, interpreted according to his own narrow bias. I can only imagine how such an unloving, fear-based judgment could be a tornado of destruction to a family unit, wreaking havoc that might never be repaired—all in the name of a Lord of Love.

I have found that correcting my consciousness of sin has, in some ways, lessened my burden of guilt for petty omissions and commissions of daily life. Conversely, it has magnified my sense of responsibility to become a ceaselessly forgiving person, which is often a far greater burden. One which, when shouldered with sincere commitment, has proven itself to be immensely liberating and empowering—that is, on the occasions when I have truly accomplished it. I have indeed learned the truth of what Jesus taught: that to forgive my neighbor is to reclaim my own power, and reclamation of personal power is closer communion with God who is, indeed, that Power itself. The only way I can be truly free is to release the chains of enmity with which I have, in my heart, imprisoned any whom I have judged as guilty.

The Commandment admonishes us to, "Judge not, that ye be not also judged." According to Judeo-Christian tradition, therefore, judgment would be construed as sin. Judgment in the sense of the Commandment must surely refer to negativity—harsh opinion or condemnation of persons or circumstances. Surely, it cannot be denied that there can be a very positive and constructive side to opinion, and anything positive should not be denied. Only in recent times have I come to fully understand the intimate relationship between judgment and un-forgiveness. They are bedfellows—synonymous, one with the other. Without judgment, there is no such thing as un-forgiveness. When forgiveness is accomplished, judgment no longer exists. In that consciousness, I have become increasingly aware of how much personal energy is lost when I judge another person or circumstance.

If energy is God expressing, the more energy I waste, the farther my ego-self feels separated from God. I cannot deny what a heavy burden it is to judge—how much judgmental behavior weighs me down. But there is often such a fine line between judgment and opinion with regard to circumstances, attitudes and behaviors. Am I not entitled to have opinions? How do I live in this world and yet be free of the burden of judgment and its dangerous destination—un-forgiveness? I now find tremendous value in becoming an observer. Increasingly, I make a conscious intent to *observe* behaviors and circumstances without forming a value—without taking a personal position or naming an opinion. "Isn't that interesting?" is a far safer position from which to think or comment upon something or someone than, "That's disgusting." In so doing, I find myself far less judgmental. I am aware I am increasingly more centered and I experience greater command of my own power. More than that, I am a happier person.

I previously suggested that without judgment there is no sin. That statement may to many seem as nonsensical as the mirthful query, "When a tree falls in the forest, does it make noise if no one is around to hear it?" I find it worthy food for thought, however. By the ego consciousness of this world, the only things sinful are those that we have judged. Again, Jesus is recorded to have said "Judge not..."

Before these words are even published I hear many readers protest, "But Jesus spoke of sin." Indeed he did. I believe we must remember Jesus was speaking 2,000 years ago to unsophisticated and mostly uneducated people. He had to reach them in language they could understand. More so, he was a spiritual renegade whose attitudes and teachings ultimately led him to torturous death. He surely had to select his words carefully in order remain in his body long enough to get his basic message across. Were he physically to walk among us today and speak to us in the language of contemporary times, I believe he would use some word other than sin. Instead of, "Go, and sin no more..." he might say something akin to, "Go, and change your consciousness," or, "Change your consciousness and change the circumstances of your life." Instead of, "Your sins are forgiven you..." he might say, "Corrected consciousness has set you free." Such semantics would not, perhaps, well serve those whose self-esteem is so low and sense of guilt so great they feel a need to be punished. It might, however, offer a banquet table of self-respect and freedom to those who are truly ready to *pick up their bed and walk* toward closer communion with God who/which is within them. "He who has an eye, let him see. He who has an ear, let him hear."

If we are each the temple of the One God expressing in, through and as us, there can truly be only one sin—the failure to recognize, embrace and express our Divine nature. That, of course includes judgment, and is, as I have grown to understand, the ultimate failure to love. All else we have called sin—murder, thievery, promiscuity, dishonesty, abusive behavior, infractions of church law, or you name it—falls thereunder and is the failure to love God our Creator, who or which is Love.

13

Poverty Consciousness

Celebrity names like Oprah Winfrey, Bill Gates, Warren Buffet, and Mark Zuckerberg are as common as dust on the top of the refrigerator (my wife's refrigerator excepted). They are a few of the most famous among the small and exclusive rostrum of America's billionaires. Each possesses material wealth beyond the imagination of most people. Yet, I doubt any one of them could or would deny their personal success began in their imagination—thoughts evolved into the granite of believing, the raw material that enabled each to sculpt wealth of monumental proportions. Oprah came from a life of abject poverty. Yet, her consciousness must surely have known and owned her Royal Divinity to have manifested such a legacy of prosperity and power. Bill Gates left an Ivy League education incomplete, and as a very young man without the coveted degree gave birth to Microsoft, and a medium of business communication that has totally changed the world.

In comparison to the vast majority of the world's people, I am and have always been, blessed with a life of reasonable comfort and privilege. Even so, I have struggled throughout my adult years to overcome poverty consciousness and I know I am far from alone. Regardless of how good things were, there was always in the back of my mind the dark little voice of "What if...the money runs out...we can't afford to take that trip...the car breaks down...we don't have enough for this, that or the other thing?" Together with his two little playmates, "I can't afford that," and "I shouldn't do that," the wicked little voice has often wreaked havoc with my sense of security, and many times rained on my parade.

Certainly it is wise to exercise prudence in the stewardship of resources. However, we cannot be conscious of our inherent divinity when such attitudes move beyond common sense and become shackles that inhibit or prevent our ability to express the unfathomable power for manifestation that is the Creator's legacy to each and every human person. Thoughts of limitation beget limitation. Doubt and fear creates more doubt and fear. Thoughts of lack generate lack. Poverty consciousness is a magnet that draws poverty.

"It is the Father's good pleasure to give you whatsoever you desire," Jesus assured us. Yet, poverty consciousness has been a prevailing attitude of Christianity for all the years of its history. Believing the promised rewards for faith and righteousness are to come in an afterlife which itself is contingent upon the extent to which we have pleased our capricious God, Christians have far too often accepted lack and limitation as though they are God's will. Yet again, we are reminded Jesus said, "The kingdom of heaven is now. Enter in." What is the kingdom of heaven? That may be up for grabs, but I believe a safe assumption is it overflows with all the good we could possibly want.

Faith in God through Jesus Christ, his only begotten Son, and the hope of endless happiness in the life after death is the force that has sustained Christians through natural disasters, wars, famine, cultural poverty, slavery, and every unimaginable demonstration of man's inhumanity to man. Such faith is powerful, and not to be disdained or minimized. Dare we even to imagine, though, how different might have been the quality of our lives as individuals, as families, as cultures, or as nations had our religious education emphasized consciousness of our God-Present Power for the here and now, rather than glorifying acceptance and endurance of the status quo in hope of something better after we move off the planet? "Offer it up," the Catholic faithful have for centuries been taught, and offer it up they (we) did, prayerfully and patiently, though their (our) hearts are wrenched with despair and their (our) faces wet with tears. How perfectly did those churches formed at the time of the Protestant Reformation follow suit?

While I doubt there was ever any ecclesiastical intent to advocate poverty consciousness as a means of behavioral/mind control, it has served that purpose well for many sectors of organized Christianity. Jesus' parable of the *widow's mite*, surely given to demonstrate our divine power to manifest through joyful giving and gratitude even from a purse that appears empty, has been a successful tool for extracting money from even the poorest of the poor in order to finance opulent palaces in which to congregate for the worship of God who is *out there*, enthroned in tabernacles of gold, or watching from the heavens above. The truth that the *Tabernacle* is within each human soul, prepared and longing for demonstration and expression of its truth and power for good has been rarely communicated. Personally, I doubt it has even been clearly understood by many faith teachers.

One of the most awesome and disappointing experiences of my life was my visit to St. Peter's Basilica at the Vatican in 1978. Humongous, vast, and beautiful beyond imagination, it is filled with art works so priceless they are worthless. Expressing my disdain to a young priest who was one of my traveling companions, I said, "We erect this in honor of a Lord who didn't even possess his own bed?!" My friend and fellow cleric empathetically responded, "It should be sealed up for a tomb." Then he said, "But we must remember that the poor Catholics of the world would be the first to come to its defense. This is their wealth." He was right, of course, even though most could never, in their wildest dreams, hope to see it. What flawed consciousness, that anyone should ever believe their wealth is outside of self, when the one in whom they have vested their trust as Lord and Savior was not arbitrary in his teaching that the Kingdom of God is within, and the Power of God is waiting for expression.

My personal understanding is that money is, like all of creation, energy, and only a tool, a vehicle of Earthly mobility, and not a measure of personal worth in any way that truly matters. Regardless, I also believe it is God's will that all—each and every one of us—should be billionaires. The Infinite and Eternal God in whom or which we *live and move, and have our being,* is a bottomless well of every resource within and beyond imagination. Only if God were arbitrary and discriminating, would He will prosperity for some and poverty for others. All have within themselves the ability to manifest good—to embrace and use their incredible, infinite power to demonstrate the good that they desire. One might imagine a person born long before the age of electricity living in a house with electric lights. Unless she knew to flip a light switch at dusk, she would remain in total darkness from sundown to sunup. No matter that the power for immediate light was there. If she did not know to turn it on it would be as though it did not exist. And, unless someone told her, or her curiosity prompted her to experiment with those strange toggles sticking through plastic plates on the walls, she would never know.

In the last one hundred years, various *new thought* philosophies have come to prominence, resulting in a wealth of enlightening and thought provoking literature to be found on the shelves of most any public library or bookstore. From such philosophies have arisen churches that focus more upon what seems to have been the religion *of* Jesus than upon the religion *about* Jesus. Prominent among them are Emilie Cady, Myrtle and Charles Fillmore, founders of the Unity School of Christianity and the Unity Church, and Ernest Holmes, founder of the Church of Religious Science and the philosophy it teaches. In our own time, celebrated teachers of *New Thought* include Dr. Norman Vincent Peale, famed author of *The Power of Positive Thinking,* Dr. Robert C. Schuller of the world renowned Crystal Cathedral in Garden Grove, California, and the popular author and teacher, Dr. Wayne Dyer. They are only a few who have heard the teachings of Jesus more clearly. They have helped to turn on the lights in the window of my soul, and have served as personal guides among others counted historically as great, master teachers.

The prosperity consciousness such men and women communicate may even have influenced some of history's greats who have risen to vast influential power as pastors of television network ministries, many of which are broadcast from huge, and often architecturally grand mega-churches. It is encouraging that some seem to genuinely provide their followers with inspiration, encouragement and tools with which to understand their intrinsic power to change unwanted conditions of their lives by manifesting good. Sadly, however, the value of the ministry is often diminished by the manner in which such faith leaders use their great influence to *extract* the widow's mite. Many and unknowable are the faithful listeners who deprive themselves of comforts, even basic necessities of life, while sending their tithes and offerings to ministers who supposedly pray for them from opulent stage settings, themselves wearing flashy diamond rings and expensive designer clothing. Later, they travel in high-end automobiles or chauffeur-driven limousines to mansion-style homes where they feast on delicacies far beyond the reach of most of their supporters.

I am reminded of a dear friend who, upon the death of her lifelong husband was left with property valued at nearly $ 1,000,000. She married again to a very sincere, good-hearted man who was steeped in poverty consciousness, and who was a faithful supporter of televangelists, several of whom have since fallen into public disgrace. Together, they gave and gave and gave, supporting the ministries of the television pastors who inspired them with hope for a multiplication of wealth, good health and happiness. After a marriage of less than twenty years, they died of debilitating disease processes, with nothing left of the material wealth they had once known. Their hearts were sincere, and their intentions genuine. Hopefully, some of their gifts accomplished good for needy and worthy causes, and hopefully their joy is great in the world of Spirit to which they went.

Who among us can measure the blessings they realized in giving so generously? Still, I know that they died in disillusionment that their fiscal fortune was gone, and their dreams not realized. How tragic that the ones who led them, spiritually fed them, did not teach them that giving, worthy as it is, requires a change in consciousness in order for the power of the Law to manifest according to its fullest potential. Writing a check while pleading to a god outside of self, rather than allowing that good to flow from the Most High that dwells within may be no less an affirmation of lack than living in an impoverished slum, and begging on the streets with a belief that such is one's immutable destiny in life.

Giving sincerely, however, even from an empty purse, with consciousness that the appearance of lack is only an illusion, knowing that the universe is a Divinely Ordered and continuous flow of infinite good that is present in all, expressing as all, for all, to all and through all, is the Divine formula for prosperity.

The late Hollywood producer, Michael Todd, is quoted to have once said, "I have often been broke, but I've never been poor." A Jew like Jesus, he obviously held Jesus' understanding that both material wealth and poverty are outward reflections of inward consciousness. One who is *broke* but fully conscious may be realizing a moment or a season of financial draught. But he or she knows the truth that such a condition is only temporary and illusory, for the power of infinity flows through self. With that consciousness, he or she possesses certain assurance that by moving one's feet in step with the orchestration of the divine, the waltz of prosperity continues.

It has often been said that you can give a man a fish and feed him for a day, but teach him how to fish and you can feed him for the rest of his life. Jesus seems to have shown us in so many ways how to change the circumstances of our life experience—not just the life of eternity, but of the present moment, the here and now. How different would have been the history of the past 2,000 years, and the quality of the untold numbers of lives who have formed it, had the truths of his wisdom—his own Divine Consciousness—been understood and communicated effectively and honestly by the guardians of Christianity? With the limitless power of such understanding to change the world, even among those who do not call themselves Christians, we might today be living in the nascent Garden of Eden.

It took a long time for me, with years of study, prayer and introspection to reform a lifetime of lame thinking, and I was well into middle age when I gained insight to begin the process of recovery from poverty consciousness. I believe Jesus proved in his work, i.e., ministry, that any condition or circumstance can be totally reversed in an instant. Alas, though, my consciousness was not yet that keenly tuned to the divine force within me. I had built up a huge fortune of negativity in my universal equity account simply by incorrect thought and word, and the dividends continued to come to me regularly and prolifically until I cancelled it with more positive investments. As I did so, I started to feel better physically and emotionally. I began to experience hope, confidence and security more than I had ever known, and I gradually gained greater insight into what Jesus meant when he said "The kingdom of heaven is now. Enter in."

I deplore some of the ploys many contemporary televangelists and congregational pastors use to *extract* dollars from their *faithful*. I find, nonetheless, a positive side to the visages of prosperity they present by their appearance and their lifestyles, and in their promises of the abundance that God has in store for those who support their ministries. They do, after all, represent more positive images than the poverty consciousness that has been too often nurtured, even glorified, by Christian faith leaders and their followers. While I believe the poor deserve our compassion and respect, and that as children of God according to any faith pathway we are duty bound to help them discover their innate power to prosper and succeed, the tradition of poverty consciousness holds them captive to the limitations of ego. It ultimately creates a drain on public resources, and contributes to a myriad of societal problems. I no longer recognize any glory in being poor, nor do I believe that such a state is God's will for us. "Our Father owns the cattle on a thousand hills," the scriptures tell us. And, "What man among you, if his son asks for a loaf of bread, would give him a stone? How much greater is the love of your Father which is in heaven!" And again, "It is your Father's good pleasure to give you the kingdom."

What encouraging, hope-filled assurances, and yet how sad it is that traditional Christianity has failed to emphasize our power and ability to receive in the here and now rather than in a far off afterlife. I believe Jesus tried to give us the keys to improve the quality of our life at all levels, spiritual, physical, mental and material, not just after death, but right here, right now. Where I have found that absent or lacking in the experience, or in the teaching of traditional Christianity, I have learned to listen, instead, to the revelations that come to me by personal communion with my Lord, and from various, enlightened teachers through whom the Holy Spirit of God continually expresses.

14

Gifts of the Spirit

The 1st Letter of Paul to the Corinthians, chapter 12, states that, "Unto some are given…" and various gifts of the Spirit are enumerated. Traditional interpretation of those verses has often been that the great puppeteer God is the discriminator whose own pleasure decides which *Gifts of the Spirit* will be given to whom. My own experience has been that such is the general consciousness of the segment of Christianity that validates contemporary expression of Gifts of the Spirit. There are, of course, the most fundamental Christian churches that believe those gifts were sealed away somewhere on the historic Day of Pentecost, and are not to be expressed again until after the Second Coming of the Lord. Personal experience of the named Gifts of the Spirit makes it impossible for me to any longer ascribe to that doctrine.

I now understand that the powers and behaviors Christians call Gifts of the Spirit are part of the indiscriminate nature of God, and are there for all who hold a consciousness to honor them and express them. In modern day business lingo, they might be called spiritual competencies. Once again I am reminded of the scripture, in its inimitable masculine form, "He who has an eye, let him see. He who has an ear, let him hear." If God is everywhere present, expressing in all, through all and as all, how then can God or would God discriminate as to the form of His expression to anyone? And, if God, among all of God's various immutable characteristics, is Divine Law, how can God discriminate as to whom He will express? Do not, once again, all get the power to burn their lamp when the lamp is connected, and isn't the power accessed in Divinely Ordered fashion?

It is irrefutable that some people seem able to express various Gifts of Spirit when others cannot. I have come to understand, however, that such is a matter of spiritual consciousness of the expresser/believer, and not according to any discriminate nature or will of God.

I grew up on the side of Christianity that believes the Gifts of the Spirit were sealed away on the Day of Pentecost. It was my good fortune to become Catholic during the Second Vatican Council initiated by Pope John XXIII, when the spirit of renewal within Catholicism included the *charismatic movement*. I began early on to attend Catholic Pentecostal Prayer meetings, and to practice those spiritual gifts, competencies, that seemed within my ability to express. In the beginning I was more than just a little *turned off* by those who demonstrated prayer tongues, or who interpreted tongues. There seemed to be an attitude among them that implied you just haven't arrived until you have a prayer tongue. I developed resistance which I expressed adamantly one evening during a visit with a very long and dear friend, a non-Catholic lady whose Protestant faith found renewal in the Catholic Charismatic Renewal, and who had become proficient in prayer tongues. It was the tonic that she personally needed, but her attitude seemed to have become such that if you didn't have a prayer-tongue you were a second class Christian. Pigheadedness seeming to be one of my most prolific spiritual gifts at that time, I dug in my heels and told her profoundly that tongues was not my gift, and that I did not want it. My limited consciousness successfully short-circuited the Divine flow and when, after the passage of at least ten years, I acknowledged that I wanted to receive and express each and every possible gift of Spirit, it was several years more before prayer tongues became part of my personal experience. I had, of course, gotten just what I had ordered up from the Divine, God, as it were, and I had to work hard to change my consciousness before that unique and very fulfilling prayer form became part of my personal faith experience.

How well I recall the night my prayer tongue expressed. It was a "Life in the Spirit" seminar at St. Francis Catholic Church in Bend, Oregon. Several of us were gathered with our hands on a brother who had asked to receive the gift of tongues. The others were singing, each in their own tongue, when suddenly I opened my mouth and began to sing in a language foreign to me. Though I had no understanding of the meaning of the words, expressing them filled me with a euphoria that seemed to lift me above the room. I had received the gift, or, perhaps, more accurately, I remembered the gift. I immediately remembered it as something I had done automatically and unintentionally as a child. From earliest memory there were times when I would be filled with the same euphoria, and I would speak or say gibberish. Since our family followed faith groups that offered no frame of reference for such activities, I thought I was stark raving mad. Every time it happened, I prayed for deliverance from the scourge. As I recall, I was somewhere around the age of twenty when my prayers were answered. I was *healed,* and my beautiful prayer tongue went into hibernation. It is just one of many instances of verification I have received over the years that we need to be very careful what we ask for.

The understanding that I have gained during many years as a practicing Christian, a Christian minister, and a recovering Christian, has caused me to know that those unique abilities that we call Gifts of the Spirit are really part of the Divine Order. It is only our lacking spiritual consciousness that limits them, discriminates among them, or totally denies their existence. Whatever anyone believes about the Divinity of Jesus as God Incarnate, or as the One and Only Son, the sacred scriptures, if they hold any truth, record that he said most assuredly that all the things He did we can do too, and even more.

As one whose life has been greatly enriched by having welcomed and practiced most, if not all, of the named Gifts of the Spirit, I am thankful, and bless the Catholic Church for opening to me the doorway to that consciousness closed by the church of my childhood. Risking the possibility that I may offend many Christian fundamentalists and charismatic elitists, I cannot deny my certainty that those same gifts and spiritual competencies are available to anyone of any faith pathway whose Divine consciousness is sufficient to know them, and to express them. How else do we explain the Universality of God, and the known ability of non-Christians to demonstrate the various spiritual gifts which literal subscribers to the sacred scriptures claim as their solitary right to posses? Again, we must ask ourselves, "Can God who is One and Universal be divided?" Clearly, for me, the answer is, "Only in the consciousness of humankind." Our Christian Gifts of the Spirit, the Spirit that is universally One, are found in non-Christian cultures and faith practices, especially among Native Americans, and un-complex tribal peoples in various parts of the world. It doesn't matter whether you're in New York City or the jungles of Borneo, if you access electricity in the divinely ordered fashion, you can operate whatever appliances or electrical devices you choose.

Years before I became involved with the charismatic renewal in Catholicism, I was introduced to the charisms of Spirit through my personal and professional friendship with Rev. Pearl Kerwin, whom I have already identified as one of my mentors. Pearl was a world-class *psychic* who had a long history of ministry to prominent movie stars of the last generation, as well as to such infamous political figures as the late FBI Director, J. Edgar Hoover. My later mentor, Rev. Howard Richards, also a tremendously psychic Christian minister, expanded my consciousness of the metaphysical realm often held in such disdain by mainstream Christianity. Granted, the world of practicing psychics is replete with charlatans of every imaginable flavor. I have come to know, however, through many such personal associations, as well as my own continually developing spiritual competencies, that the capacity to *read* another person's energy field, or the energy grid of a particular culture or society, is nothing more or less than what was happening with the prophets of the BIBLE, and their respective prophecies.

The BIBLE speaks of spirits and their manifestation to the physical realm, this third dimension reality that we call Earth life. We casually and suspiciously talk of ghosts and haunting, but mainstream Christianity looks askance at spirit manifestations, often regarding those who see or communicate with them as ones who hobnob with the *devil*. I, however, as well as untold numbers of other totally sane persons who fear to speak as openly as I, have seen, heard, and experienced disembodied persons, souls, entities—call them what you will.

One of my earliest and most dramatic experiences occurred about thirty years ago when I was only a *novice* at non-religious, spiritual encounters. My mother's cousin Edward died of a gunshot wound to the head when I was about ten years old. It was known that Edward was associated with some men of questionable integrity, but the cause of death was ruled suicide, a most grievous concern to his family which, because of their very fundamentalist Christian faith, considered suicide an unforgivable sin, punishable by eternal damnation. I had not thought of Edward, or heard others speak of him for more than twenty-five years when, at the age of thirty-five, I was shaving before my bathroom mirror on a Saturday morning. I don't recall what I was thinking at the time, but certainly nothing related to what was about to occur. Suddenly, Edward's image appeared in my consciousness and his voice spoke into my right ear, saying, "I want my mother to know I did not kill myself. I was murdered."

I was totally stunned, but had no doubt as to the validity of what I had just experienced. I immediately went to the telephone and called my mother who had learned to trust my unfolding psychic abilities, as well as her own. Her Aunt Myrtle, Edward's mother, was in her late eighties by that time, and had always been troubled about Edward's salvation and safety in the life of Eternity. Among his ten siblings, there was one sister who my mother knew had the consciousness to understand and accept the spirit communication I received. Mom called her cousin Marybelle, who went directly to her mother and explained the marvelous, hope-filled contact from Edward. It made a world of difference in the quality of the remaining two or three years of Aunt Myrtle's life on Earth. Why and how did Edward come to me to convey that message to his mother? I can only presume that it was because I was the first person in his family of origin whose consciousness had become sufficiently *tuned* to receive his vibration.

I was a teenager when my grandmother, my mother's mother,

desperately needed help with a situation in her life that my mother knew nothing about. One night my mother was awakened from her sleep by the presence of her own grandfather, her mother's father, who returned to spirit when Mom was a small child. Her grandfather, who in life always called my mother *sister*, said, "Sister, help her." My mother inherently knew that the message concerned her own mother. She began the very next day to determine the nature of the problem, and ultimately provided the help my grandmother needed.

In the chapter on miracles I discussed a few of the spontaneous healings I have experienced, both as the receiver and as the medium, or channel. I well recall, as a child, the tent revivalists who traveled the country saving souls, casting out demons, and healing sick minds and bodies. I was about nine or ten years old when a few successful revivalists began moving to the living rooms of America through the wonderful new medium called television. An aura of mystery always surrounded those productions, together with an often comical display of emotion and theatrical dramatics. I remember sitting with friends and laughing at the alleged healers, and at those claiming to be healed. Like practicing psychics, there were many charlatans—down right fakers, among them. There was also a lot of sincerity and good, old-fashioned faith. Some of those ministers were pure-hearted practitioners, despite their, often questionable, private lives, and, among those who came forth to be healed were many who received their heart's desire.

I had a great uncle, now in spirit, who was one of the kindest, gentlest men I have ever known. A no-nonsense kind of guy, and not particularly religious, he was supremely intelligent and not given to indiscriminate emotion. As a very vital, young man, Uncle Frank was stricken with rheumatoid arthritis. Receiving the limited medical therapy that was available for that condition more than eighty years ago, he was facing a life of severe limitation and discomfort when the infamous evangelist Amy Semple McPherson came to Douglas, Arizona, with her traveling tent revival. Though Amy's ministry was a bit before my time, I have read many accounts of her work, and spoken with numerous people who remember her, as well as some of her personal relationships, which were often disdained by *God-fearing* Christians. Uncle Frank was somehow moved to take a chance, and he went to that healing revival. He entered the tent, walking on a cane, and left carrying that same cane, which my cousin, his daughter, still has in her possession. Uncle Frank worked his entire lifetime as the foreman of railroad section gangs, was no stranger to hard work, and lived into his eighties.

How did such a healing occur? Who can say for certain? My personal experience of such things, however, assures me that a discriminate God somewhere out there in the universe did not say, "I like this man. I think I'll grant his healing request," and then turn a less compassionate eye to others. Somehow, the ego barriers of a channel named Amy Semple McPherson, and a receiver called Uncle Frank dropped their guard enough for the God in them both to unite in expressing the desired outcome. There was unity—synchronicity—serendipity. Uncle Frank's body was healed. How? Some things we just have to accept at face value, without explanation. I only know that it happened, and I know that I know that it happened.

I have had similar experiences, and have known far too many stalwart, credible persons, not as brave or as vocal as I, who could attest the same. Jesus said, and I repeat it again, "All that I have done, you can do also." Why has the Christian church for 2,000 years tried so fervently to keep us in darkness concerning our inherent, personal divinity, and the great power it holds? Is it a legacy from the years when the hierarchy of the church held temporal power over the lives of people, even entire governments and cultures—both the faithful and the unfaithful? Is it not far more difficult to enslave or control people when they are in touch with their personal power and know its source is within them? Is it ignorance, even among those most educated, the pedagogues of scripture; or is it fear to consider any possibility beyond the party line?

One of my most memorable experiences of the world of Spirit involved my younger son, Patrick, when he started first grade. Unlike his elder brother and sister who delighted in trips with their grandparents, and who easily made the transition to school life, Pat was very much a homebody. He didn't want to be away from home unless it was with his parents. A child with exceptional intelligence and quiet disposition, he was perfectly happy in his own space, with the things and people most familiar to him. Having to leave home and spend most of the day in school was a traumatic experience for Patrick. He cried at bedtime from Sunday night through Thursday night. The crying began again when he awoke in the morning, and continued when his mother left him at school. It was heart-wrenching for parents to see their normally happy child so broken-hearted, and became quite frightening when after three or four weeks, he ceased to eat properly and began to lose weight.

The day that he went AWOL from school and walked more than a mile home alone whisked his mother and me into a state of near panic. After putting a sobbing child to bed that night, we prayed together for help. Patrick's bedroom doorway was directly across the hall from our own, and the window adjacent to his bed was covered on the inside with slatted, wood shutters. Just before dawn, his mother and I were awakened by a loud sound as though someone had run their hand down the slats of the shutters. Wondering what Pat could be doing, and intending to investigate, we both rose up in bed. Just as we looked toward the bedroom door, a very dapper little gentleman walked out of Pat's room. He had wire rimmed glasses and a goatee. Dressed in striped pants with a vest and cutaway coat, he sported a distinctive, gold watch fob and carried a black bag like an old-fashioned country doctor. When our eyes met, he smiled at us, nodded respectfully, and walked on down the hallway as though he was heading for the front door. We both knew instinctively that he was a physician from the world of Spirit, and we felt such peace and reassurance that we lay back down and fell briefly into a most restful sleep. When the whole house awoke a short time later, Patrick was happy, laughing, and seemed anxious to go to school. From that day forward, attendance at school was a priority for him, and he was a superior student. My wife and I cannot deny what we experienced.

Prophecy was one of the most respected and revered competencies in Biblical times, and there are entire books in the BIBLE that record the teachings and activities of the prophets of old. After the Christian church rose to power, however, prophecy was included with the spiritual gifts sealed away on the Day of Pentecost. It was as though pre-Pentecostal prophecy was validated, and any that came after Pentecost was suspect, if not the work of the devil. Granted, many persons of questionable authenticity and selfish intent have marketed themselves as psychic counselors, astrologers, intuitive, etc. There have been many, though, even in current times, who are honorable, sincere, and authentically gifted prophets who, through a variety of unique mediums, are able to foresee future events for an individual or culture. Some read an energy grid. Others have spirit guides who speak to them. Some get images or information from unknown sources. Personal ego, the human condition, can distort or cloud information received so that nobody is 100% accurate. However, many there have been and still are whose intuitive perceptions have been verified, and are acclaimed. Perhaps the most famous was the 16th century, French seer Nostradamus, whose prophecies are still scrutinized, contemplated and popularly publicized.

Many remember the world-famous astrologer, Jeanne Dixon, a resident of the Washington D.C. area, who is reported to have pleaded more than once with President John F. Kennedy to change his plans and not go to Dallas in November 1963. She had foreseen the assassination that awaited him.

I have referred several times to my late and dear friends, Rev. Pearl Kerwin and Rev. Howard Richards, both of whom were for many years appreciated by my family and friends for their authoritative, visionary counsel. My wife and I are currently blessed with a very dear friend named Lynda Diane, a counselor in metropolitan Phoenix, Arizona, who is as authentic and true as any I have ever known. A psychic medium of world renown, her quiet, non-sensational ability to intuit for her clients is unequaled in my own experience. Lynda Diane's personal competencies are held in such high esteem that she has actually been retained by agencies of the U.S. Government and by various law firms to assist in their official interests, often of a classified nature. She takes calls from all over the globe for eight to twelve hours a day, and the positive difference she makes in the lives of her clients is immeasurable.

John of God

My most life changing experience with spiritual competencies surrounds a man in central Brazil who millions of devotees throughout the world affectionately call Joao de Deus, or in English, *John of God*. Perhaps the world's most renowned, contemporary spiritual healer, Joao Teixeira de Faria is, since his youth, credited with immeasurable healings of every kind imaginable. Joao is a man whose work in many ways mirrors Edgar Cayce, the famed *Sleeping Prophet*, who lived and worked in Virginia Beach, Virginia, during the first half of the 20th Century, Joao differs in that he is a conscious medium. In a self-allowed, trans-state, Joao vacates his body and allows powerful *Entities* from higher dimensions, the *world of Spirit,* to speak and work with hopeful pilgrims who come in search of spiritual growth, and healing for physical, mental, and emotional infirmities. The approximately forty known Entities that the Medium incorporates include known physicians long gone from this Earth, historical greats such as King Solomon and King David, and revered saints of the ages such as Saint Ignatius of Loyola, Saint Francis, and Saint Raphael.

John of God receives pilgrims at his spiritual hospital called the Casa de Dom Inacio, the *House of St. Ignatius,* named for its patron saint who directed Joao to found it more than thirty years ago on a specific site adjacent to the village of Abadiania in central Brazil. The Casa welcomes people of every faith, and of no particular faith, and they come by hundreds of thousands every year for spiritual healing, to experience the interventions that the Medium offers without requirement of compensation. Documented healing accounts, many examined and verified by medical authorities, are innumerable, and they fail to include an even greater number, such as my own, that are undocumented but shared openly and joyfully with all who will listen.

The personal experience of Oprah Winfrey and her staff has generated significant attention to the Casa de Dom Inacio through various dimensions of Oprah's media interests during the past several years. Even Dr. Wayne Dyer, one of the foremost self-help authorities of contemporary North America, has gone viral with an inspiring YouTube account of his personal healing of leukemia through the non-local intervention of the Entity incorporated in Joao de Deus.

Personal experiences with John of God have accomplished such profound healing in my own life that I petitioned Casa officials for recognition as a designated Group Leader, and I now take seekers from the United States to experience the wonders of the spiritual gifts expressed through the Medium and the Spirit Entities he incorporates. I am privileged here to share a few of those most notable with you.

I met my dear friend Dessa on my first trip to the Casa de Dom Inacio. A high-spirited, vibrant, European woman who was at that time in her middle 40s, Dessa struggled with a lifetime of depression and emotional pain that she attributed to an oppressive, Catholic childhood in the home of two very negative-minded parents. A most tragic event involving her paternal, great grandmother seemed to have had a karmic effect upon her grandmother, her father, and ultimately, her sisters and herself. Again, I am reminded of the sacred teaching that "The sins of the fathers shall be visited upon the sons unto the seventh generation." Having struggled for so many years with a heavy burden of emotional pain, Dessa was having suicidal ideation when she learned of John of God and the Casa de Dom Inacio. She voraciously searched the Internet for all the information she could accumulate and, having never before traveled to Brazil, found herself two weeks later in the village of Abadiania with nothing but her suitcase, her pain, and her hope. Dessa went before the Entity incorporated in John of God, bearing a petition for help for her relentless depression before she destroyed herself. Spiritual intervention was offered, and she was sent to her room to sleep for twenty-four hours, as is the customary protocol.

Dessa and I first cast eyes on each other as we were leaving our adjacent rooms, both having just risen from the prescribed, post-intervention slumber. Her blue eyes dancing, with a smile as broad as her face, she was one of the most joyous, vibrant women I have ever known, and remains so to this day. We are both now Casa Group Leaders who meet up in Brazil once or twice each year, and her joy only gets better as the years pass. I recall her email to me several months after our first meeting when she wrote that her parents kept asking her when she would be herself again. She said to me, "Randy, how do I help them understand that I am not the person they tried to form me to be, and they'll never see that person again?"

Kevin and his wife Catherine, also friends from my first trip to the Casa, are from Ireland. Kevin had been diagnosed by physicians with end-stage prostate cancer in August of the previous year, and advised to get his affairs in order because he had no more than two months to live. As he was proceeding with doctors' instructions, one of Kevin's daughters learned of John of God through a friend, and said "Dad, I think you should look into this." After quick investigation, Kevin and Catherine, lifelong practicing Catholics, boarded a plane for Brazil within ten days. Kevin experienced an extraordinary two weeks at the Casa, and returned home to Ireland feeling quite well. Not only did he not die, his health consistently improved. The following February Kevin and Catherine returned to the Casa for another wonderful two weeks. In June, his physician ordered a complete medical workup. Kevin smiled from ear to ear when he recalled the afternoon he sat across from his physician's desk while the doctor scrutinized the medical record for fifteen minutes, repeatedly exclaiming, "Hmmm! Hmmm!" Presently, he looked up and said "Kevin, I don't know what you're doing, but keep it up. There is no evidence of cancer anywhere in your body." A convicted believer in the gifts of the medium in Brazil, I met Kevin on his third visit to the Casa in twelve months.

Lisa is a successful professional woman in her 50s who traveled with me on one of my trips to the Casa last year. She was raised by two emotionally abusive parents and has no remembrance of love from them. She has struggled throughout her life with self-esteem issues, and had for many years been medicated for bi-polar disorder. After her twenty-year marriage disintegrated, she became so depressed that she cried nearly all the time, and found herself barely able to function. She went to John of God a skeptic, but so desperate that she was willing to try anything. During her two weeks of interventions at the Casa her symptoms first magnified so dramatically that I wondered whether she would make it. By the end of the second week, however, all in my group became aware of a shift in her demeanor, even though she seemed to feel nothing. By the time we returned home she was feeling that shift. To see her now is total delight. A tall, handsome woman, she stands proud and carries herself with confidence. Her smile is infectious, and her energy radiant. To hear the testimony she bears of her life-transforming experience with John of God is total joy.

Among the various pilgrims I have taken to the Casa de Dom Inacio, the most remarkable is surely JoAnn, a woman in her early seventies who joined my last pilgrimage, five months ago. A successful business-woman of the cyber age, JoAnn imports custom merchandise from a Central American country and markets it through seventeen of her own E-bay stores. At the time of our Casa trip, JoAnn was feeling some uncertainty as to future choices, and the only intention she took to John of God was a request for help in discerning direction for the remainder of her life. With a spirit of openness and total acceptance, she became subject to an entire litany of wondrous events that began even before she reached the Casa, and that continue even unto this present day.

The week before we left for Brazil, JoAnn injured her right shoulder. Though medically undiagnosed, the symptoms were much akin to the torn rotator cuff for which I have had surgery, and she boarded the plane in Phoenix with considerable pain and limitation in her range of motion. Somewhere on one of the two flights between Phoenix and Brasilia the pain went away. JoAnn reached Brazil with her shoulder totally healed.

The first time JoAnn went before John of God, the Entity incorporated told her she needed to lose weight, and said, "We will help." By the time she left the Casa ten days later she had already lost twelve pounds without altering her diet in any way, and the pounds continue to disappear.

A diabetic requiring daily insulin therapy, JoAnn discovered after one week at the Casa that her blood sugar was normal, so she withheld her medication. After returning home her physician confirmed that the diabetes was no longer present, and recommended that insulin be permanently discontinued.

Prior to our departure for South America, a lesion on her face was diagnosed as squamous cell carcinoma, and her physician wanted to surgically remove it. JoAnn refused, and the cancer disappeared during her time at the Casa.

For the better part of a year prior to our trip, she had experienced an uncomfortable and unsightly rash on her lower legs and arms. Her doctor was unable to accurately diagnose the condition, and none of the recommended medications seemed to make any difference. That, too, became history at the Casa, as well as swelling in her ankles and legs.

The product of an unhappy childhood with an unloving and hyper-critical mother who had died only the previous year, JoAnn had for her entire life carried a bag of emotional pain. She left that bag at the Casa, and now acknowledges understanding for her mother, rejoicing that she has forgiven her totally.

Other remarkable healings include her blood pressure, which re-turned to normal, and remains so, a hissing sound in her ears has gone away, she no longer falls down stairs, and she seems to have developed an immunity to stressful conditions that surround her.

Shortly after her return to Phoenix, JoAnn began to experience posi-tive changes of an entirely different nature. Business challenges seemed to evaporate before her eyes, and money flowed consistently and easily. If she had a need, she would simply say, "God, do your thing," and the need was filled. She then began to notice that whenever she was in the presence of friends or business associates who themselves were experi-encing lack or challenges, their circumstances reversed within a matter of two or three days. She became known as the *lucky penny*.

JoAnn's most phenomenal demonstration occurred three months af-ter her healings at the Casa. Her brother-in-law, an Islamic man from an eastern culture, lay dying in a hospital in the United Kingdom. Several months prior he had received a kidney transplant, which, though suc-cessful in every other way, led to an infection that traveled throughout his body, and settled in his brain. He was unconscious, non-responsive, and on a ventilator, and his physicians had recommended removal of life support. JoAnn called me to ask whether we might petition the Spirits of the Casa to help sustain him until her husband could make the long trip from Phoenix to London to be with the family as his brother died. I had her provide me a photograph of her brother-in-law, which I emailed to a friend at the Casa with a request that the desired petition be taken before the Entity incorporated in John of God. Her husband had not yet flown when the following morning his sister called to say that the family had grievingly encircled their brother's bed, believing him to be dying, when suddenly he moved a leg and started to show signs of awakening. The days that followed were, themselves, a litany of seemingly incredible circumstances. He totally awakened, regained full use of his body, started speaking again, and soon regained his memory and his ability to reason. A couple of days after he first awoke they were preparing to take him down to dialysis, since his new kidney ceased to function when the infection took over. Before dialysis, however, he urinated two times, a pretty sure sign of a functioning kidney. Though still hospitalized, the recovery continues daily, and JoAnn calls me whenever there are new positives to report. Her husband's devoutly Islamic family continually praises Allah, and gives thanks to John of God, and the Entities he incorporates.

The most recent, wondrous event in JoAnn's life surrounds her husband's granddaughter in Pakistan. The child was born with genetic anomalies and physicians told her parents that she would only be here for a brief time. At nine years old, she stands only thirty-eight inches tall, and suffers weakness and general malaise. She is hyper-sensitive to sunlight, and cannot tolerate the light of day without her eyes shielded. One of her most distressing symptoms, though, has been severe, general unhappiness. It is reported that she has not found any cause to feel happy for a very long time. Just one week prior to this writing, JoAnn sent me a picture of the child, which I sent by email to the Casa with a request that a petition in her behalf be taken before John of God. On the day of presentation, the Entity incorporated in the Medium said "I will visit her tonight." The result has, so far, been astounding. The child is happy, growing stronger each day, and enjoying going out onto the veranda in the sunlight. What a wonderful healing for her and her family, despite whatever length of time she may remain with them.

JoAnn goes about every day with tears streaming down her face, constantly mindful and joyously thankful for the blessings she knows. The most beautiful thing about her story is the very clear affirmation that God, by whatever name, is One, without bias for persons or religions.

As I gather my next two groups of pilgrims for the Casa, one two months from now, and another two months following, I am witnessing the healing power of God and intervention of members of the world of spirit right here in my own community. Cheryl, the thirteen-year old daughter and only child of devoutly Catholic parents was diagnosed slightly over one year ago with cancer of the hip and thigh. Bones were removed and replaced with prosthetic substitutes, and it was hoped the problem was solved. Before long, though, the cancer traveled to a lung, which was removed, followed by traditional cancer therapy. About two months ago, the cancer revealed itself on her chest wall, and the medical community advised her parents there was nothing more that could be done, and they should prepare themselves to give her up. That same day, her father was laid off from his work, a very mixed blessing. The unfortunate event made it possible for him to be home, and totally present to his wife and daughter. It created financial hardship, however, which they least needed at such a frightening time. The family began to search for help beyond the traditional medical community, and learned of a renowned intuitive and hypnotherapist in another city to which they quickly traveled. There, they were introduced to the possibility of reincarnation as Cheryl submitted to past life regression. New possibilities opened for each of them, far beyond their traditional Christian training, and when they returned home Cheryl was confident that she would beat the disease process, and totally committed so to do. They connected locally with an energy worker with whom I associated and, though Cheryl's commitment remained strong, her body declined. She had barely eaten for two weeks, when the energy worker asked if I would accompany her on her next bi-weekly visit. I agreed, but asked first for a picture of the patient that I could transmit to the Casa for presentation to John of God. The picture arrived at the Casa the day before I first met Cheryl. That afternoon while the energy worker pursued her therapy, I simply laid my hands on various points of Cheryl's body for slightly over an hour. The report that came on the following day was astounding. The good news started when she ate a full supper that night. Cheryl had already begun to meditate, and both parents joined her in that prayerful activity. Her mother was also sleeping in the same room with her. That first night her mother turned out the light, and they planned to meditate together until sleep. After a short while, Cheryl exclaimed, "Mom, the room is filled with angels, and they're seven feet tall. There are four of them working over me right now. One of them tells me his name is Vincent, and that he has been with me in many lifetimes. He tells me I will get well, that the cancer will be gone within three months, and that I will be myself again in six months." She also said "Vincent tells me they are working with you, because you carry a lot of emotional pain over my disease. He also says there are two angels upstairs working with Dad, and he says that Dad will back at work within three months."

When I went back to visit Cheryl the following week, she and her parents told incredible stories of continued communication with the spirit world. Her mother said that every night she would lay and listen to her daughter interact with the angels. Sometimes she would talk. At other times she might say things like "Ouch. That hurts." On night she just laid and murmured all night long. On two occasions during that week Mother Mary came to Cheryl. Radiantly clothed, Cheryl could not see her face, but was conscious of a beautiful smile, and the radiation of energy that was indescribably warm and loving. Cheryl had continued to eat, and was gaining strength. She was going back to school in a wheelchair the next day, but only for one day. Vincent told her she must not return to school full time for the next month. As of this writing, the marvelous healing continues right on schedule, and that beautiful family continually offers thanks for the wondrous healing, and for the expansion of their consciousness surrounding the truths of life and the infinite Power of God.

How wondrously blessed I feel to intimately witness such powerful demonstrations of the vast possibilities, even realities, that abound in a sea of infinity for those who dare to step outside the lines drawn for them by traditional Christianity.

This brief discussion of the so-called Gifts of the Spirit barely scratches the surface of known reality and possibility. Those who have experienced God in deeper, more mystical ways than traditional worship, beautiful and fulfilling as it may be, and who have dared to look, listen and think outside the various boxes of dogma and ecclesiastical authority, know there is a vast universe of unfathomable possibilities within us and around us. Dr. Robert Schuller, of the Crystal Cathedral, always encouraged his readers and his audiences to be *possibility thinkers*.

I have never met Dr. Schuller, but I would welcome the opportunity for a heart-level visit with him. My sense is that he personally knows, has even experienced, possibilities far beyond those known by his faithful congregants. The *Christ*, though totally encompassing, is expressed as a sliding scale in each according to his or her own consciousness at any given time, and is often expressed as the competencies sacred scripture of Christianity calls *Gifts of the Spirit*. I now believe Jesus, my Lord, my brother and my best friend, to be the first to realize the fullness of the Christ consciousness. Rev. Pearl Kerwin, who loved him dearly, and who always called him Lord, also called him *the first completed soul*. Who can say with certainty? I only know that the Jesus I know intimately from scripture and from personal association is not totally the same Jesus taught to me by the various denominations of Christianity by which I have been influenced. I believe there is the Christ of each of us according to whatever degree we recognize and express it. I wish I had a dollar for every person who has revealed to me that is also the truth they hold secretly in the secure silence and safety of their own heart.

15

Eternal Destinations

I wonder how many Christians grew up, like me, in fear and trembling of the *theological place of eternal punishment*—hell. From the pulpits of good-hearted, well-intentioned pastors we were threatened weekly with never ending anguish in the lake of fire and brimstone somewhere beneath the surface of the Earth if we didn't repent of our sins and die in a state of grace. Woe unto those who were not saved. Their doom was sealed. That included all who had not professed their faith in Jesus Christ and been baptized according to the *Trinitarian Formula*—"in the name of the Father, and of the Son, and of the Holy Spirit." In many Christian denominations the list of the damned also included *so-called* Christians who did not believe righteously, or worship correctly. I can remember, have even in my later ministry experienced, those whose faith was so founded in the fear of Satan and the fires of hell that it's hard to imagine how their consciousness had room for the love of God.

Those who gained God's favor, and whose name was found in Saint Peter's Book of Life, were at death given passage through the *Pearly Gates* of heaven where they went before the throne of God the Father, with Jesus the Son sitting at his right hand. White gowns, angel wings and harps were distributed, and all sang and praised God forever and ever, amen. The Catholic tradition included, still does, a preliminary step for all those destined for the choirs of heaven. They must first go to a place called purgatory where they are purged, or cleansed of their sinfulness in order to become worthy for presentation before the throne of the *all forgiving and totally loving* God. Many, but not all, Christians have now come a long way from such archaic, mythical images, yet, most do not have any credible certainty of what death and the afterlife may afford.

There is, irrefutably, scriptural basis for common, traditional concepts of heaven and hell. The visions of John in the Book of Revelation vividly describe the throne of God, the angelic presence, and the proverbial streets of pure gold, as well as unthinkable devils, demons and excruciating, eternal anguish of the underworld. Jesus himself spoke of the *fires of gehenna*, and warned of judgment and damnation for those who were not found worthy. We are again well to remember, however, that Jesus was trying to raise the consciousness of spiritually ignorant people. Had he not spoken in the language and imagery of the time, he could not have reached any of them. Gehenna was a name given to the fires that burned outside the walls of cities and villages surrounding the area where Jesus lived and taught. Such places would have equated to our modern-day city dumps where people take their garbage. The fires burned unceasingly, consuming the waste material, which they were fed. They were also a place that received the bodies of executed persons—those deemed not worthy of decent burial. What a perfect allegory that presented for the future destination of wasted souls—those who were not in favor with God at the time of their death.

Change has always been the only constant in this Earth life, and Death would appear to be the ultimate and greatest change. All humans go through life knowing that someday they will die, and along the journey, most know the sorrow of having loved ones plucked from their embrace by the proverbial *Angel of Death*. Much of Christian understanding about the death experience seems to flow from the wealth of mythology and folklore of the pagan cultures that passed before us. More than twenty-five years of my life having been dedicated to spiritual health care, however, with a strong focus on death ministry, has afforded me understandings for which most people have no frame of reference. The things I know are formed from my own observance of those experiencing death, and from the information given me by those who were privileged to leave their bodies and return, commonly called the *near death experience*, to which I will hereafter refer as an NDE. I welcome this opportunity to briefly share.

Regardless of how death occurs, whether peacefully or traumatically, I have come to understand that it is like stepping out of one's trousers or dress, and leaving the garment lifeless on the floor. A similar analogy is an automobile that has movement because the driver operates it. When the driver pulls it to a stop, turns off the ignition and gets out of the car, that vehicle demonstrates no life or mobility. It sits dead and still. The driver, however, is just as alive, and when he or she leaves the car has greater mobility than the automobile afforded. We are spiritual beings having a physical experience here on planet Earth. The body is simply our vehicle and, being mortal, cannot live without the spirit in it. The spirit, however, needs no physical body, and is just as alive without it. The spirit is, after all, Divine—an extension and an expression of God. The eyes of the soul open simultaneously when the eyes of the body close for the last time.

I have often known dying persons to speak of the unbelievable LIGHT that comes to them when death is imminent, or when they were experiencing an NDE. It is described as gloriously bright, beautiful, and encompassing. When preparing people to die, I learned to tell them to watch for the LIGHT, and when it came to simply step out of the body and go into it. The LIGHT did not always seem to be there for those who were spiritually unconscious. In all my years, however, I only had one patient describe to me a negative or frightening NDE. That man found himself out of his body and in total darkness. He felt cold and alone. Jesus spoke of those living in darkness, and he referred over and again to the LIGHT. He also made it clear that heaven is available to us now, on this Earth, in these bodies. "Enter in," He entreated us. I have come to believe, therefore, that the presence of the LIGHT when we leave our bodies is contingent upon OUR presence to the LIGHT while we are in our bodies. Those who, by their consciousness, live in the LIGHT, remain in the LIGHT when they cross into spirit. Those living in the dark may pass into darkness. God, however, cannot be divided, and all are created in the "image and likeness of God"—Divine Presence, as it were. Therefore, all will, must, eventually find their way to the LIGHT. As Rev. Pearl Kerwin taught, the doorway to reformation is never closed. Still, it's a vast, very black universe out there. I personally do not want to enter it in darkness.

Death is, more than physical, an energetic experience whereby the individual moves from one dimension into another. Those who pass into the LIGHT often speak of a tunnel, or some sort of channel through which the spirit travels to other planes of life—higher realms of existence. I find it interesting that the proverbial tunnel is depicted in religious art dating to the middle ages of history, yet, those who have never seen such works often seem to have a similar experience. I have rarely spoken to a person who entered into the LIGHT who did not either see or go part way into the tunnel. Some went clear through to the other side.

I remember my own grandmother who in her middle eighties fell and broke her hip. During her hospitalization I stopped every day to see her on my way home from work. One day she was in a bit of an altered state, and very disgruntled, as only she could be. "Where is that tunnel?" she demanded. Having knowledge of the tunnel, and knowing that she, a lifelong fundamentalist Christian, did not, I asked, "What tunnel?" "What are you talking about?" "That tunnel!" she replied most emphatically. "It was here just a minute ago, and now it's gone." I knew, of course, that she had passed very near the point of transition to another plane of life. She didn't understand what the tunnel was, but she knew instinctively that she was to go into it, and she felt frustrated and cheated that it seemed to have gone away. When the call came three years later that she had died, I was the first family member to arrive at the Intensive Care Unit where she had been treated. I remember standing over her still warm but lifeless body, and thinking, "Praise God! She finally found the tunnel?"

My own mother had an interesting tunnel experience prior to her death. She was mostly bedfast, and often in a somewhat altered state of consciousness. She did a lot of reminiscing during those days, and spoke of interesting visitations and experiences that, though somewhat irrational from the perspective of *Earth consciousness*, were clearly of the spiritual dimension. My wife sat by her bedside and listened, often taking notes. Mom described seeing a culvert, something like the large, metal tubes that are often used in road construction to provide a passage for excess water to flow from one side of the road to the other. She spoke of looking into the culvert, and she could see children playing at the other end, looking back at her. Knowing that she had most probably seen the transition tunnel, Joan asked her whether she went into the culvert. Mom replied "Oh, no. That's dangerous. You mustn't go in there." Five weeks later she went suddenly into the tunnel and did not return.

Many people I have known have visits from spiritual beings as the time of their death draws near. Some describe angels, the *Blessed Mother*, or Jesus. Others speak of visits from loved ones who are already in spirit. I have stood often at the bedside of dying persons who, though unconscious, suddenly awakened and exclaimed, "Mother!" "Dad!" or, the name of some other beloved, departed person. Mom had repeated visits from her own mother during the five weeks leading to her transition. When visitations occur from spiritual teachers or faith leaders, it seems to be in accordance with the individual's particular spiritual consciousness or faith tradition. Whereas a Christian might see Jesus, or Mary, his mother, a person of another faith might see a prophet, teacher, or Lord of their own consciousness—Krishna, the Buddha, Mohammed. Let us herein remember the words of Jesus. "I have other sheep that are not of this fold," and, "In my Father's house there are many dwelling places."

One of the most extraordinary accounts of such visitations surrounded my wife's grandmother, Viola, whose husband, Roady, died forty-four years previously, leaving her to finish raising their five sons alone. Gramma, lived in a large, mid-western city in which her eldest son, my father-in-law, lived afar, on the opposite side. He faithfully visited her weekly. Several weeks before her death, my father-in-law stopped to see his mother, a very no-nonsense kind of person, who said, "Robert, your father was here today." My father-in-law thought, "Oh, boy! She's losing it." He humored her with, "Is that right, ma? And what did Dad say?" She replied, "He stretched out his hand and said 'Come, Viola.'" "Is that right, ma?" my father-in-law said, "And what did you say?" She replied, "I said 'No Roady. I'm not ready yet.'" The scenario was repeated several weeks later. It was identical, except Roady said "The next time I come, Viola, you will come with me." A couple of weeks following, Gramma suffered an early evening heart attack and dropped suddenly and finally to the floor. In her BIBLE she had written on the morning of that same day, "November 1, 1974, this will be my last day on Earth."

Gramma made a rather spectacular return when she visited her eldest great granddaughter, our niece Joani who expresses considerable psychic aptitude. Joani wears Gramma's gold wedding band, the inner surface of which carries an engraving of the date Viola and Roady were married, March 13, 1914. On the evening of March 13, 2012, Joani was getting out of the shower when she suddenly saw Gramma standing there, pointing to the hand on which the ring is worn. Gramma then laughed, laughter that Joani was able to hear. When Joani later reflected upon the experience she realized that the month and day, March 13, was the same as that engraved on the ring. It was Gramma's 98th wedding anniversary

Seeing spiritual beings or disembodied persons is not just a phenomenon associated with those nearing death. Many perfectly sane persons have such experiences; often choosing not to speak of them for fear of ridicule, or not trusting the validity of their perception. Some who are steeped in conservative fundamentalism consider it the work of Satan. I was five years old when I first remember seeing a spirit, whom I later learned was a great grandmother who was gone long before my birth. I have known people of high spiritual consciousness such as my friends Rev. Kerwin and Rev. Richards who saw spirits frequently as they went about their daily work and leisure. My wife has become accustomed to seeing spirits from time-to-time as she performs her domestic tasks. For others, it is an exceptional experience that occurs at a time of stress, or extreme personal need.

I have known several people who are accustomed to seeing a

departed person sitting in the congregation at his or her own funeral. One, a very quiet, non-demonstrative minister of exceptional integrity in the African Methodist Episcopal Church always looks for the disembodied soul, and says she often finds him or her smiling, as if delighted at the service of remembrance that is taking place in his or her behalf. Rev. Kerwin told me that the day she made the decision that her own body was to be cremated was the day she was conducting a funeral service and, looking down from the pulpit, watched the spirit diving into the casket and careening back again. The disembodied spirit apparently did not have the consciousness to go forward into the LIGHT, and was trying to re-enter the body that would not, could not, receive it.

During the latter years of my ministry I often recommended the movie *Ghost*, to those struggling to understand the phenomenon of death. The film had something for everyone—suspense, humor, romance and inspiration. While there were parts that I know to be unrealistic, such as the ugly demons coming to drag the soul of an evil-behaving person off to hell, there was, nonetheless, *more truth than poetry* in the way the death experience is described, and the endurance of the soul thereafter. Those who have seen it will recall that at the end the spirit of the man played by Patrick Swayze says to his beloved, played by Demi Moore, "All there is, is love." What a beautiful way of saying, "God is all there is!"

The preceding paragraphs contain only a few of the personal experiences and associations that have formed my consciousness about the death transition, and the survival of the spirit after it leaves the body. What happens beyond that is part of the great unknown, even though many have been privileged to see glimpses of that which we call eternity. Some survivors of near death experiences who have gone into the tunnel and returned give interesting and hope-filled accounts of what is on the other side. My own experiences, together with those of immeasurable others, attest, however, to a vast community of life within the body and without he body, on this planet and beyond. Knowing the little that we do, can we even fathom the possibilities that may exist, here and hereafter?

I love the story that is told about a man who died and found himself before St. Peter at the Pearly Gates. St. Peter found the man's name in the Book of Life, but told him that the rules of heaven require that before anyone can enter in they must go down to hell to see what life is like there in order to make a truly *informed consent* as to whether they really want to spend eternity in heaven. The man suddenly finds himself down in hell, and in the presence of a demon that ushers him into a giant banquet hall where dismal, gaunt, starved-looking people sit at long tables heaped high with every imaginable, delicious kind of food. The man is seated between two of the unhappiest looking people he had ever imagined. He turned to one and said, "I don't get it. There is all of this sumptuous food before us, yet everyone looks as though they are starving, and there is not a smile in the place." The other person responded, "There is this silly rule down here in hell. Everyone has to eat with four-foot-long chopsticks, and nobody can figure out how to use them," the man said. "Oh, I don't like that. I want to go back up to heaven." When he arrived back at the Pearly Gates he assured St. Peter of his certainty that heaven was the place where he wanted to spend eternity. St. Peter, thereupon, ushered him into a huge banquet hall that looked exactly like the one he had just left behind in hell, except that the people were all plump, rosy-cheeked, and laughing. When he had been seated, he turned to the person next to him and said, "I can't believe it. I just visited hell and found that they have the same wonderful banquets down there, except that they're all starving and miserable because they have to eat with four-foot-long chop sticks." His neighbor laughed and said, "Oh, we have the same rule here in heaven. We've just learned how to feed one another."

It is, of course, only a story, much akin, perhaps, to the wise and beautiful imagery Jesus gave us so prolifically. Imagine, however, what would be the quality of our lives, here and hereafter, were we all to learn the same lesson.

I cannot describe the peace of mind that enveloped me when I finally came to the understanding that there is no hell, apart from temporary states of negative consciousness that we create for ourselves. A disciple of reincarnation, as I have already established, I, like many others, have gleaned insights from hypnotic regression into past lifetimes.

There remains, however, an unfathomable realm of possibility which none of us can define. The certainty, for me, is that God is, and that life is eternal, all life, proven to me by animal spirits I have seen. Jesus knew all this, and I truly believe he was trying to communicate that beautiful hope to the people he loved in the only words, images and parables that their *primitive* minds could understand. "He who has an eye, let him see. He who has an ear, let him hear."

16

The Second Coming

"Christ has died, Christ has risen, Christ will come again," is a Memorial Acclamation repeated by faithful congregants during the Roman Catholic Mass. Beyond what I believe to be the flaw that implies the name Christ as synonymous only with Jesus, it bespeaks expectation of the return of our Lord to the Earth. That consciousness is consistent with those Protestant Christians who also await the return of Jesus in a glorious phenomenon named *The Rapture*. In the words attributed to Jesus in the Gospel of John wherein He spoke to his disciples of his forthcoming ascension into heaven, He is reported to have said, "I will come again to take you with me, that where I am you also may be." The disciples, of course, expected that return to occur during their own lifetimes, and Christians have lived for 2,000 years with the same expectation. Though not specifically stated in the BIBLE, fundamentalist Christians have, from implications of several references in various Biblical books, developed a tradition of expectation that the Lord will return in a *blaze of glory*, and the saved of Earth will be caught up to meet him in the air, then be whisked off to a place called heaven. The *unsaved* will be left behind. That event is similar to parables of Jesus wherein he described the *Great Day of the Lord* when two neighbors will be working side by side, and one find the other suddenly gone: a day when the sheep and goats, the righteous and the unrighteous, will be gathered into the master's barn. The righteous will be found worthy, and be admitted to the *Kingdom of Heaven*, and those judged unworthy will be cast down to the place prepared for the devil and his angels.

As graphic and frightening as these images may be, I have found peace and confidence in my understanding of the creation and evolution of sacred scripture, and in the remembrance that Jesus, even if quoted correctly, was trying to help spiritually primitive people to comprehend eternal truths; that in so doing he had to use language and imagery with which they could identify. Had my grandmothers both of whom came west in covered wagons, been told they would live to see on their television (what the heck is that?) a man step out of a spaceship (Huh?) and walk on the Moon, they would have thought the message bearer was stark-raving mad. They had first to grow in experience and con- sciousness before they could understand and validate such a seemingly impossible feat. Had anyone living prior to the age of electricity and telecommunication been told of my laptop computer and the Internet that I travel daily, they would neither have understood nor believed it. I sometimes have difficulty believing it, myself. Any good teacher knows that to help people grow in consciousness you must be willing to start with them at the place where they are, to walk with them at the pace they can travel, and to instruct them in language they can understand. Jesus is known to many as the Master Teacher.

When I combine faith, common sense, reason and experience, a formula that terrifies many Christians and threatens many theologians, I determine that the *Second Coming of Christ*, like salvation, occurs every time one of God's *children*, whatever the faith tradition or lack thereof, grows in spiritual consciousness—ascends to a higher level of Divine LIGHT—picks up her bed and walks. Whenever the universal Christ becomes magnified in a person, by virtue of that individual's choice or willingness to grow in spirit, it is *Rapture*. The Lord comes again, and again, and again as every soul becomes more conscious of its Divine nature—an extension of the One, Infinite and Eternal God. How often have I been left behind as those beside me grew in spiritual consciousness? How often have I left behind friends and loved ones who held to a consciousness that prevented them from going with me when I *ascended*?

With every graduation of our own spiritual consciousness, we move higher, progressing toward full realization of the Christ that is both our Divine legacy and our true nature. Jesus said in the Gospel of John, "In my Father's house there are many dwelling places…" The context in which He was speaking to his Apostles is traditionally accepted as a reference to the life of eternity. The same words seem to fit, however, for our spiritual consciousness, personal and collective. In our Father/Mother God, there are many places where our consciousness may dwell. A few verses later, Jesus is reported to have said, "I will come again and take you with me, that where I am you may be also." What a beautiful and reassuring invitation to each and every one of us to grow in our own Christ consciousness, that we may attain the Divine Mind of Jesus.

It is unfortunate, I believe, that in the Christian tradition we are not encouraged to strive for the mind of Jesus. Most definitely, He is established as our foremost example. Be like Jesus, we were taught when we were children. Live only the way Jesus would want you to live. Refrain from those thoughts and behaviors that would not please Jesus. "What would Jesus do?" is the contemporary catch phrase of many Christians. Those may be inspiring standards to offer little children in Sunday school classes, but it is an impossible goal to attain without the mind of Jesus. How different would be the quality of our lives, were we as individuals to attain the mind of Jesus, whatever our personal religion or lack thereof? We can only imagine what a different place this world would be if only one in every 100,000 persons realized and expressed the Christ consciousness as fully as did Jesus.

As one who has known intimate, personal experience with Jesus the entity, the Lord of my own life, I now believe that, in truth, the second coming is our own ascendance to the Christ consciousness. On that great day, whether in this incarnation or one yet to come, we will each, in our own time, become One with the mind of Jesus—our Divine legacy and the truth of our very being as the illusion of ego evaporates away and we *remember* our Oneness with God.

17

"Seek Ye First the Kingdom of God..."

"...and all else shall be added unto you." Most of us, it seems, spend our entire lifetime seeking. We seek freedom. We seek recognition. We seek validation. We seek wealth. We seek fame. We seek the perfect mate. We seek perfect health. We seek work. We seek leisure. We seek joy. We seek forgiveness. We seek hope. We seek friendship. We seek adulthood, and then we seek youth. We seek, we seek, we seek... Our seeking would fill an entire book, and then some. How often do we either fail to find that which we seek, or, when we do find it, we determine that it is not enough, or that it is not what we think we want?

Jesus gave the perfect formula, the Divine formula, for fulfillment of our every need. "Seek ye first the Kingdom of God and His righteousness, and all else shall be added unto you." I wish I had a dollar for every time I have heard a minister or faith teacher in church, in Sunday school, or on TV, expound upon his or her formula for fulfillment. Study the scriptures. Pray like hell. Send your money to my ministry. Go to church faithfully every time the doors are open. Refrain from sin, which can include anything from extramarital sex to smoking, drinking alcohol and coffee, or wearing makeup but, sadly, it far too often does not include refraining from judgment.

There may be value in some of those do's and don'ts of faith practice, but they conveniently bypass the formula the Lord gave. "Seek ye first the Kingdom of God..." How did he tell us to do that? Go within. "Go to your Father in secret, and your Father will hear you." What are we to suppose Jesus did during the forty days and nights when he withdrew into the wilderness to fast and pray? He surely didn't spend all that time on his knees, hands folded and head bowed, pleading and begging to a God who already knew all his wants, needs and fears. More so, if he *was* truly the one and *only begotten Son* of the Father, he would have known all things and been fully reconciled to the fate that awaited him. I believe that Jesus, though he was divine, and perhaps the most spiritually evolved soul who had ever been born to this planet, may have known that he, too, was still unfolding. He was seeking even closer and deeper communion with God who dwelt within him—within us all. His forty days of prayer must have been mostly meditation—a turning inward and a journey upward to higher consciousness. He may have been, as the Buddha would have called it, still unfolding—on the path to total *enlightenment.*

How many are the years that I have sought the meaning of life; fulfillment of self in things, concepts, philosophies, religion, worship, sacraments, or people? How faithfully have I kept ecclesiastical law without attaining the peace, the hope, the answers I needed, and the fulfillment for which my soul longed? Many of those are valid and integral to a joyous, confident, and happy life. None, however, is the be all and end all. They are components and by-products, rather than the end product.

The end, I have come to understand, is total communion with the Source—God who dwells within all, and expresses through all and as all. That the glorious, Divine Presence is obscured in most of us, perhaps, in all of us, most of the time, is only the illusion of our own false creation previously identified as ego—the kingdom of self—an unconscious and irresponsible expression of our personal Divinity. Those who live near the seas are well familiar with the marine layer, fog, which often forms over the waters and coastal areas during the hours of darkness. In the morning, it can seem as if the sun has lost its power. Always, however, the sun has its way and does all it knows how to do—express light and warmth to planet Earth. True to its own illusive nature, the marine layer goes away, for it cannot long exist in the warmth of sunlight. So it is with ego. When we understand it for what it is and begin to look beneath it for truth, the illusion loses its power, and we regain ours. I have come to understand at the very core of my being that Jesus was trying to awaken the people he loved from the slumber of their ego consciousness, and lead them to the LIGHT.

In seeking the Kingdom of God, I have often felt as though I was grappling, hacking my way through some dense jungle. At other times I found myself in peaceful valleys, or at the warm shores of gently lapping waters. In the joy of worship, the emotion of prayer meetings, and the experience of various Gifts of the Spirit, I have ascended to mountaintops so high, and skies so blue and clear that I was sure I could see forever. Just as quickly I have found myself in valleys so deep, dark and ominous that I felt immobilized by fear and trembling. Truly, there have been times on my spiritual journey when I, like Jesus, cried out, "My God, my God, why have you forsaken me?" I doubt there are many Christians whose common experience of faith has been otherwise; except, perhaps, those who have attained such levels of mastery that they inherently remain still, no matter how threatening and turbulent the appearance, and go within to the Source of their own being for protection and victory.

Those who study and track disastrous storms—tornados and hurricanes—know that at the center of every storm is a void, a vortex, a place of total peace and calm. It is only through the development of a committed, daily discipline of meditation that I have come to understand what I believe Jesus knew. It is surely what the mystics of Judeo-Christianity knew, still know, and, before them, the mystics of the eastern religions and philosophies. It is simply this: when you know the location of the *Kingdom*, you are always safe and never alone, even though you seem separated from it by the illusion of ego and all its silly little fear-filled manifestations and mantras. Whatever the ego-consciousness of the world hands us, I have come to know that victory is certain and unfailing. It is surely the consciousness that enabled Jesus to willingly enter Jerusalem at the Feast of Passover, knowing that his journey would lead him to Gethsemane and Golgotha.

For me, the scriptural account of Jesus' forty days alone in the desert describes a perfect avenue for seeking the Kingdom of God. Prompted, even goaded, by our churches, we have become so accustomed to *doing* in order to get there. Go to church. Read the BIBLE. Pray often. Keep the Commandments. Live justly and righteously. Take this seminar, or that workshop. Receive the sacraments. Give your tithe, and don't forget your offering. Little emphasis is given, though, to simply *being*. The pulpit messages of our ministers often surround the wonderful Beatitudes, *Be Attitudes* outlined by Jesus in the Gospel of Matthew, each one worthy in its own right.

I must personally confess many bypassed opportunities, however, to use my position of prominence in the pulpit to lead the faithful to the place where God can best be found—the still and quiet center of themselves; to encourage them, or show them, how to develop a committed discipline for simply *being*: being quiet, being still, being alone, being free of all thought and distraction, being in the present moment, being conscious of the infinite and immeasurable power within me. Why? Because I, like so many other sincere and dedicated teachers didn't really know. I was teaching of and praying to a God *out there*. I did not understand that so long as I was chattering my fervent praises and prayer requests, it was difficult, often impossible, for me to hear the voice of God who dwelt within me, gently and lovingly caressing the strings of the harp of divine knowledge, that most sacred *Arc of the Covenant* that lies deep within me—within all.

"Be still, and know that I AM God." Jesus, my own Lord and Master Teacher knew, as did the Buddha, Mohammed, Krishna, and surely other messiahs not of my experience, that the Kingdom of God is within us. Our religions, our churches and our temples can be beautiful and wonderful vehicles, and our faith leaders worthy companions for our personal journey to the Kingdom, so long as we do not place our power and authority in them, or allow them to become our destination.

The destination, even within the parameters of this experience called Earth life, cannot be contained or charted by any ecclesiastical institution or dogmatic philosophy. The true compass and best navigation system for finding that destination is the example of Jesus. Go within to the place where the Presence of God most dwells, and longs most profoundly to express. Were each and every human person on the face of this Earth to simply, "…be still, and know that I AM God," linking elbows around the globe as an outward sign of that universal, inward grace, there would no longer be a destination on this planet, or beyond. We would already be there. "Seek ye FIRST the Kingdom of God…" (the place where God can be found) "and all else will be added unto you." "The Kingdom of Heaven is now. Enter in."

18

Alpha and Omega

On the physical plane of existence, every beginning has an ending, and every ending is a new beginning. It is so beautifully demonstrated in our own solar system, whose planets and stars continually spin, and rotate around one another in Divinely Ordered orchestration. That cosmic drama is played out in measurement of Earth time that we have named the calendar. Every twenty-four hour period brings daylight, darkness, and returning daylight. The days progress into seasons—spring, summer, fall, winter, and the return of spring. So it has been since time immemorial, and so it continues like a spinning wheel, again, and again, and again. A seed is planted in the soil. It germinates in Divinely Ordered fashion and gives forth a root. A sprout forms, and grows upward toward the light of the sun. In its own time it bears fruit, a vegetable or a flower with its own seed that falls back to the soil, and the process is repeated season after season, after season.

How can we observe such synchronicity and not know that there is an unseen Force—benevolent and immutable—a universal maestro of the orchestra, which or who directs it all? More so, I have come to understand that the maestro IS ALL—the director and the directed, the instrument and the player, the singer and the song. That every member of the orchestra sometimes plays out of key—probably always plays out of key—and that many fail to tune their instrument, or to read the music, or to look at the director's baton in no way denies the reality of the orchestra and its director. The miracle, or so it would seem, is that the song, despite all the sour notes, is always beautiful, and without end.

How did it all come to be? Even if there was a *Big Bang*, and there may well have been one, *jillions* of years ago, how could it possibly have fallen into such perfect, synchronistic order without a motivating Divine Presence? Where can it possibly lead? How do we explain all of the metaphysical realities that vast generations of perfectly sane people have experienced, even though condemned or discouraged by orthodoxy? How do we place our total authority and power in a book that came to be through such flawed channels, and affirm its priceless value as an immutable handbook for life?

What about well documented, widely experienced, psychic phenomena, aka, *Gifts of the Spirit*—visions, prophecy, spiritual entities, bi-location of the body, healing, the power of thought over physical matter?

How do we explain the fact that the highly respected, academic and scientific discipline that we call Quantum Physics is in every definable way synonymous with metaphysics—the spiritual science? And, how do we explain the fact that an almost unbelievable number of the world's most esteemed Quantum Physicists are men and women of high spiritual consciousness, often practicing members of one or another of the world's various faith traditions?

Who can know, within the illusory and ever changing consciousness of present time? Alpha and Omega—the wheel continues to turn, and I now understand that the individuals we believe ourselves to be turn with it, again, and again, and again. We are components of it. We are it, for God is All-ness, and we are all part of God. And, for each present moment, we must be content with the certainty that whatever we know, we know nothing. The possibilities are endless, and the unseen reality is so vast, so unfathomable that the total experience, the mass consciousness of the world from the beginning of recorded time would fit on the fingertip of the Eternal Divine. The 13th Chapter of 1st Corinthians, the revered *love chapter*, declares it so perfectly: "Now we see through a dark glass…but then we shall know, even as we are known."

I know, and I know that I know. What I know most certainly is that in the infinite scope of all there is to know, I know nothing except that GOD IS—therefore, I AM.

Epilogue

What does it mean to be a Christian? Surely, I am not the only one who has struggled with this huge question that ecclesiastical authority—the Christian church—has not satisfactorily answered, for me, at least. I still cannot be certain. Through the process of seeking, however, opening closed doors that were often forbidden, walking alone on thin ice, diving head first into dark, seemingly bottomless waters, and swimming upstream against raging rapids, I have determined for myself what it is not. It is not membership in any particular ecclesiastical body that claims to alone be vested with the whole truth. It is not allegiance to any power or authority that beats a drum to which I must march, dictating when and where I am to step—right face, left face, about face. It is not any philosophy or body of knowledge that closes the curtains to the windows of my soul, and dispenses fear to contain me. It is not judgment of those who identify with God—Jehovah—The Divine—The Force—Higher Power, in ways we do not understand. It is not exclusion of those who do not look like us, talk like us, or think like us.

My personal truth is now that to be Christian is to seek and hold the universal, divine consciousness that was so imminently and immensely expressed in the historic and eternal Jesus of Nazareth who is my best friend—the Lord of my life. That consciousness and the truth it encompasses may be defined in diverse ways by people of other cultures, or be integrated into their faith experience in the same way much of the wisdom of the Buddha is reflected in the teachings of Jesus. My own truth is that to be Christian is to strive continually for closer understanding of, and communion with God who dwells within me, and within all, which is clearly the teaching of Jesus. It is also my own truth to claim my mystical, personal Divinity, and seek to express it openly, honestly, justly, and always in love.

I have always loved to go to church. Liturgical music, especially the beautiful, old southern gospel hymns on which my early faith was nurtured, flawed as their theology may now appear to me, still stirs the depths of my soul. I treasure the sacred scriptures, even though I may not always hear them in the same way as the *party line*, or as they are delivered by whichever minister is leading worship. Sacred ritual such as that present in a well-celebrated Catholic Mass brings me peace and comfort. I bask in the warm presence of other souls who form the congregation, some seekers, and some followers—some, free-spirited dancers, and some, marionettes. I delight in an inspiring, stimulating, truthful, and joy-filled sermon or homily. Sadly, they are often far too scarce. One of the advantages however, of the hearing loss that often accompanies advancing age is that I can always turn off my electronic ears.

Most of all, I love Jesus. I have for as long as I can remember, and I cannot imagine life without him. He is my Lord. My religion, though, might now be called the consciousness *of* Jesus, rather than the religion *about* Jesus. I AM commissioned by his instruction—"Seek and you shall find," but don't be fooled by appearances ("Judge not.") "He who has an eye, let him see. He who has an ear, let him hear." "I AM [is] the way." "The Kingdom of Heaven is now. Enter in."

About the Author

Rev. Randol Batson, is an internationally acclaimed leader in new paradigms of spiritual healthcare. A lifelong Christian privileged to work professionally with persons of diverse cultures and faith pathways, his experience of God and the spiritual dimension of life has grown far beyond the parameters of organized religion and ecclesiastical dogma. Retired and living with his wife, Joan, in Sun City, Arizona, Randy is now an author, motivational speaker, personal counselor, spiritual medium, and certified Group Leader for the world renowned Spiritist hospital in Abadiania, Brazil, the Casa de Dom Inacio, to which he takes seekers for healing through the intervention of the legendary trans-medium known as *John of God*.